Israel in the 1973 Yom Kippur War

Dedication
To all of the Israel Defense Forces soldiers
who fell in the war

Israel in the 1973 Yom Kippur War

DIPLOMACY, BATTLE, AND LESSONS

DAVID RODMAN

sussex
ACADEMIC
PRESS
Brighton • Chicago • Toronto

Copyright © David Rodman, 2017.

The right of David Rodman to be identified as Author of this work has been asserted in accordance with the Copyright, Designs and Patents Act 1988.

2 4 6 8 10 9 7 5 3 1

First published 2017 in Great Britain by
SUSSEX ACADEMIC PRESS
PO Box 139
Eastbourne BN24 9BP

SUSSEX ACADEMIC PRESS
Independent Publishers Group
814 N. Franklin Street, Chicago, IL 60610

All rights reserved. Except for the quotation of short passages for the purposes of criticism and review, no part of this publication may be reproduced, stored in a retrieval system, or transmitted, in any form or by any means, electronic, mechanical, photocopying, recording or otherwise, without the prior permission of the publisher.

British Library Cataloguing in Publication Data
A CIP catalogue record for this book is available from the British Library.

Library of Congress Cataloging-in-Publication Data
Names: Rodman, David, author.
Title: Israel in the 1973 Yom Kippur War : diplomacy, battle, and lessons / David Rodman.
Description: Brighton ; Chicago ; Toronto : Sussex Academic Press, [2017] | Includes bibliographical references and index.
Identifiers: LCCN 2016028847 | ISBN 9781845198329 (hardback) | ISBN 9781845199517 (paperback)
Subjects: LCSH: Israel–Arab War, 1973—Influence. | Israel–Arab War, 1973—Diplomatic history. | Israel–Arab War, 1973. | Israel—Politics and government—1967–1993. | BISAC: POLITICAL SCIENCE / International Relations / Diplomacy. | HISTORY / Military / General.
Classification: LCC DS128.185 .R63 2017 | DDC 956.04/835694—dc23
LC record available at https://lccn.loc.gov/2016028847

Typeset & designed by Sussex Academic Press, Brighton & Eastbourne.

Contents

Acknowledgments	vi
List of Abbreviations	vii
List of Illustrations	ix

Introduction: The Historiography of the Yom Kippur War   1

Part I   Diplomacy

1. The American–Israeli Relationship   13
2. The Israeli–Jordanian Relationship   25
3. Nuclear Arms, Deterrence, and Compellence   33

Part II   Battle

4. Israeli Combined Arms Warfare   41
5. Israeli Resurgence on the Golan versus in the Sinai   59
6. Israeli Airpower in the Six-Day and Yom Kippur Wars   71

Part III   Lessons

7. The Impact of American Arms Transfers to Israel   89
8. The American Assessment   97
9. The Israeli Response   113

Conclusion: From Defeat to Victory in the Yom Kippur War   125

Notes	129
Bibliography	157
Index	163

Acknowledgments

A number of the chapters in this book are based upon previously published work. Chapter 1 is a revised and expanded version of a chapter in one of my earlier books, *Arms Transfers to Israel: The Strategic Logic Behind American Military Assistance* (Brighton: Sussex Academic Press, 2007). I would like to thank editorial director Anthony Grahame and Sussex Academic Press for granting permission to draw upon this earlier chapter. Chapters 2 and 7 are updated versions of the following articles, respectively: "Friendly Enemies: Israel and Jordan in the 1973 Yom Kippur War," *Israel Journal of Foreign Affairs* 6/1 (2012), and "The Impact of Arms Transfers to Israel during the 1973 Yom Kippur War," *Israel Journal of Foreign Affairs* 7/3 (2013). I would like to thank editors Laurence Weinbaum and Yvette Shumacher for extending permission to make use of these articles here. Chapter 4 is a revised version of "Combined Arms Warfare: The Israeli Experience in the 1973 Yom Kippur War," *Defence Studies* 15/2 (June 2015). I would like to thank editor David J. Galbreath for granting permission to include this article here. Chapter 6 is a revised version of "The Israel Air Force in the 1967 and 1973 Wars: Revisiting the Historical Record," *Israel Affairs* 16/2 (April 2010). I would like to thank editor Efraim Karsh for extending permission to incorporate the article into this book. Chapter 8 is a revised version of "Eagle's-eye View: An American Assessment of the 1973 Yom Kippur War," *Intelligence and National Security* 31/4 (June 2016). I would like to thank editor Loch K. Johnson for granting permission to make use of this article here. And I also would like to thank the journals division of the Taylor & Francis Group, <www.tandfonline.com>, for extending permission to include articles from the aforementioned journals in this book. Finally, I would like to thank the Israel Government Press Office for granting permission to reprint photos from its National Photo Collection in this book.

List of Abbreviations

AAA	Antiaircraft Artillery
AEW	Airborne Electronic Warfare
A'MAN	Israeli Military Intelligence
APC	Armored Personnel Carrier
AWACS	Airborne Warning and Control System
C^2	Command and Control
C^3I	Command, Control, Communications, and Intelligence
CAS	Close Air Support
CIA	Central Intelligence Agency
DEFCON	Defense Condition
ECM	Electronic Countermeasures
FPB	Fast Patrol Boat
GHQ	General Headquarters
HQ	Headquarters
IADS	Integrated Air Defense System
IAF	Israel Air Force
IAFC	Israel Air Force Center
IASF	Israel Air and Space Force
IDF	Israel Defense Forces
IN	Israel Navy
MAC	Military Airlift Command
NATO	North Atlantic Treaty Organization
NPT	Nuclear Nonproliferation Treaty
NSA	National Security Agency
NSC	National Security Council
PGM	Precision-guided Munition
PLO	Palestine Liberation Organization
POL	Petroleum, Oil, and Lubricants
SAC	Strategic Air Command
SAM	Surface-to-Air Missile
TRADOC	Training and Doctrine Command (United States Army)

LIST OF ABBREVIATIONS

UAV	Unmanned Aerial Vehicle
UN	United Nations
USAF	United States Air Force
VISINT	Visual Intelligence
WP	Warsaw Pact
WSAG	Washington Special Actions Group

List of Illustrations

Illustrations appear after page 78. All are reproduced courtesy of the Israeli government and/or the individual photographers.

1. Israeli aircraft during a "show of force" flyover before the Yom Kippur War.
2. Israeli tanks and mechanized infantry moving on the Golan.
3. Israeli aircraft overflying mechanized infantry on the Golan.
4. Israeli artillery firing on Syrian forces on the Golan.
5. Israeli tanks advancing in the Sinai toward the Suez Canal.
6. Israeli commanders conferring in the dunes of the Sinai.
7. Israeli fighter-bomber taking off for a sortie over the Sinai front.
8. Israeli tanks crossing over the Suez Canal on an Israeli-constructed bridge.
9. Israeli troops inspecting captured Egyptian surface-to-air missiles (SAMs) on the Egyptian side of the Suez Canal.
10. Israeli fast patrol boats (FPBs) at anchor before the Yom Kippur War.
11. Members of the Agranat Commission at their first meeting to assess Israel's war effort.

Photo Credits
1: Moshe Milner; 2: Eitan Harris; 3: Unknown; 4: Ze'ev Spector; 5: Ilan Ron; 6: Yossi Greenberg; 7: Moshe Milner; 8: Unknown; 9: Gad Binter; 10: Moshe Milner; 11: Ya'acov Saar. All photos © Israel Government Press Office.

Introduction
The Historiography of the Yom Kippur War

During the afternoon of October 6, 1973, Egypt and Syria launched massive simultaneous assaults against Israel in the Sinai and on the Golan, respectively, thus triggering the Yom Kippur War, the fifth major round of interstate hostilities in the long-standing Arab–Israeli conflict.[1] Initially caught off guard on both the northern and southern fronts, the Israel Defense Forces (IDF) suffered painful reverses in the early days of the conflict, while the Syrian and Egyptian armies registered some impressive accomplishments. Within the first week of the war, however, the IDF had not only stopped the Syrian army in its tracks, driving it back to the prewar border, but the IDF had also launched a counteroffensive of its own into Syria proper that would quickly bring it to the gates of Damascus, the Syrian capital. By the end of the second week of the war, the IDF had smashed the Egyptian army's attempt to break out of its bridgeheads in the Sinai in order to reach the narrow mountain passes and had crossed over to the Egyptian side of the Suez Canal. And, by the middle of the third week of hostilities, the IDF had completely surrounded one of the two Egyptian army corps involved in the fighting, advancing to within a hundred kilometers of Cairo, the Egyptian capital.

Diplomatically speaking, the Yom Kippur War constituted a turning point in the Arab–Israeli conflict. Despite experiencing yet another military setback at the hands of Israel, the Arab world had its "honor"—lost in the utterly humiliating defeat of the 1967 Six-Day War—restored as a consequence of the opening days' achievements in the war, especially the Egyptian army's crossing of the Suez Canal. This salving of the Arab ego, combined with postwar exhaustion on both sides, allowed the United States to broker disengagement agreements between the major protagonists. The fulfillment of these

1

agreements, Egypt's desire to solidify its relationship with the United States, and the fear of renewed Soviet meddling in the Middle East on the part of both Egypt and Israel, in turn, led directly to Egyptian–Israeli peace negotiations, which culminated in the signing of a peace treaty in 1979. The often tense Egyptian–Israeli relationship notwithstanding, not only has the peace treaty survived to the present day, but it also eventually served as an example to encourage other Arab states and nonstate entities to negotiate with Israel. Jordan and Israel signed a peace treaty in 1994, while the latter has intermittently held talks to settle its disputes with Syria and the Palestinians, albeit without much success to this point in time.

Militarily speaking, the Yom Kippur War ended in a clear victory for Israel, a quite remarkable achievement in light of the circumstances that obtained at the outset of the fighting. But its victory had been a very expensive one. The IDF lost over 100 aircraft, at least 700 tanks, up to 75 artillery tubes, and more than 2,500 soldiers, including a large number of officers. Arab losses—mainly Syrian and Egyptian, but also Iraqi, Jordanian, and other—were much greater. Collectively, Arab forces lost 400–500 aircraft, 1,500–2,000 tanks, about 500 artillery tubes, and more than 15,000 soldiers.[2] Indeed, American military officers expressed shock and dismay at the rate at which fighting machines had been destroyed in the Yom Kippur War, noting that North Atlantic Treaty Organization (NATO) forces could not long sustain a conventional war effort against Warsaw Pact (WP) forces in central Europe if faced with similar expenditures.[3]

Rather predictably, then, the Yom Kippur War has attracted a significant amount of attention over the years from a range of informed observers. Descriptions and analyses of the war itself, as well as of its diplomatic and military antecedents and results, are not in short supply. Soldiers, diplomats, journalists, historians, political scientists, and so on in Israel and the Arab world have produced a constantly expanding list of volumes about the war in Hebrew and a somewhat smaller corpus in Arabic in the decades since 1973.[4] The present literature review, however, focuses specifically on the books that are available to an English-speaking audience—and it makes no claim to be comprehensive even in this regard. The point here is not to catalogue all of the many volumes thus far written about the origins, course, and consequences of the Yom Kippur War, but instead to survey a range of the most important and informative works in order to get a sense of what has been researched to date. Such a review serves to illustrate how this book will help to fill certain lacunae in the literature about the war.

The Diplomatic Historiography of the Yom Kippur War

Journalists published the first books to tackle the diplomacy surrounding the war. Edward Sheehan's *The Arabs, Israelis, and Kissinger* and Matti Golan's *The Secret Conversations of Henry Kissinger* are representative of this species.[5] Both books, as announced by their titles, purport to tell the story of American diplomacy, especially in the aftermath of hostilities, when the United States fulfilled the role of "honest broker" between Israel and the Arab states, leaving the Soviet Union out in the cold. Sheehan, an American, essentially endorses the thrust of that diplomacy, while Golan, an Israeli, portrays it as largely anti-Israeli and pro-Arab. Mohamed Heikal, who served as an official spokesman for the Egyptian government for many years, supplies his country's point of view about diplomatic developments before, during, and after the war in *The Road to Ramadan* and *The October War*.[6]

Beginning in the late 1970s, historians, political scientists, and diplomats began to add their own voices to the chorus. Historian and diplomat William Quandt surveys American policy during the Yom Kippur War in *Decade of Decisions*, while political scientist Michael Brecher, who pioneered the analysis of Israeli foreign policy, scrutinizes Israeli decision making before, during, and after the fighting in *Decisions in Crisis*.[7] Written long before the declassification of Israeli and American documents about the Yom Kippur War, Brecher's analysis has stood the test of time quite well. Similarly, the analyses offered in political scientist Alan Dowty's *Middle East Crisis* and political scientist Steven Spiegel's *The Other Arab–Israeli Conflict*, both of which concentrate on the American perspective, as well as political scientist Shlomo Aronson's *Conflict and Bargaining in the Middle East*, which examines events from the Israeli perspective, have also stood the test of time nicely.[8] While none of these five books looks exclusively at the Yom Kippur War, all of them manage to cover the war in substantial depth.

Diplomats brought out at least two important books about the Yom Kippur War in the 1990s and early 2000s. Soviet diplomat Victor Israelyan presents unique insights into Soviet decision making during the war in *Inside the Kremlin During the Yom Kippur War*, illustrating his country's confrontational policies vis-à-vis the United States.[9] In *The October War*, Richard Parker, an American diplomat with much experience in the Middle East, compiles contributions by American, Soviet, Israeli, and Arab diplomats, military officers, historians, and political scientists, essentially allowing them to discuss the background, course, and consequences of the war from their individual perspectives.[10]

INTRODUCTION

Historians, political scientists, and diplomats alike have usually tended to perceive the Yom Kippur War as an outgrowth of the results of the Six-Day War in particular and the 1967–73 interwar period in general, and the opening of national archives has only accentuated this line of reasoning. The opening of archives in the United States, Israel, and, to a lesser extent, Russia has permitted historians and political scientists to probe the origins of the war as never before. Notable in this regard are *In Search of a Peace Settlement* by political scientist Moshe Gat, *The Nixon Administration and the Middle East Peace Process, 1969–1973* by political scientists Boaz Vanetik and Zaki Shalom, and *1973* by political scientist Yigal Kipnis.[11] All three of these volumes make extensive use of American and Israeli archives in an effort to determine whether the United States could have brokered some sort of peace agreement between Egypt and Israel during the interwar years that would have averted hostilities between them in 1973. Historian Craig Daigle also makes extensive use of government documents in *The Limits of Détente* to show how the Yom Kippur War can be attributed, at least in part, to the functioning of the American–Soviet relationship.[12] On the topic of official documents, mention must also be made of the *Foreign Relations of the United States* volume that covers the Yom Kippur War.[13] This collection of documents is indispensable to an appreciation of American policy during the war. Henry Kissinger, Secretary of State at the time, reproduces some of the same documents in *Crisis* to reflect his (somewhat slanted) take on American diplomacy during the war.[14]

A few other works that touch on the diplomacy of the Yom Kippur War are worth noting here as well. Though the contributions in *Revisiting the Yom Kippur War* are not mainly focused on diplomacy, political scientist P. R. Kumaraswamy incorporates a couple of meditations on Israeli and Soviet policies surrounding the war.[15] Like Kumaraswamy's volume, political scientist Asaf Siniver's *The Yom Kippur War* is not dedicated entirely to the diplomacy of the war; however, it contains contributions on American, Soviet, Israeli, Arab, and European policies, as well as a contribution on the role of Middle Eastern oil in the war.[16]

The Military Historiography of the Yom Kippur War

Like many armed conflicts of the past, the Yom Kippur War has given rise to a slew of battlefield histories of varying quality over the years. Among the first wave, two by Israeli observers deserve special mention:

October Earthquake by Ze'ev Schiff and *The War of Atonement* by Chaim Herzog.[17] Schiff, long the doyen of Israeli military correspondents, effectively weaves together general commentary about hostilities on the Golan and Sinai battlefields with personal accounts of individual IDF soldiers caught up in the maelstrom. Herzog, a former head of Israeli military intelligence (A'MAN) and, later, president of the State of Israel, meticulously traces the progress of the war on both fronts, and devotes a separate chapter to the fighting in the air and at sea. Herzog's volume in particular has stood the test of time with respect to its general accuracy about and insight into the war. While a number of other, lesser-known Israeli observers also penned works about the Yom Kippur War in the years following the hostilities, their counterparts in the Arab world remained curiously silent, at least in English.

Shortly after the publication of this first wave of books about the war, soldiers on both sides of the divide began to get into the act. Avraham Adan's *On the Banks of the Suez* describes his division's part in the fierce battles on the Sinai front.[18] The always controversial Ariel Sharon, a fellow division commander on the Sinai front, tells his (and his men's) story in *Warrior*.[19] Both Adan and Sharon rather candidly lay out—each from his own point of view—the command problems on this front that beset the IDF throughout the war. In *Dado, 48 Years and 20 Days*, journalist Hanoch Bartov recounts IDF Chief of Staff David Elazar's management of the Israeli war effort.[20] Though Elazar received much of the blame for the IDF's unpreparedness prior to the outbreak of the war, Bartov's work makes clear that his subject typically proved to be a level-headed wartime manager who guided Israel's armed forces to ultimate victory. A tank battalion commander during the Yom Kippur War, Avigdor Kahalani offers a gripping account of how his unit completely stymied the Syrian army's assault in the northern sector of the Golan in *The Heights of Courage*.[21]

Like their nonmilitary counterparts, Arab soldiers have been less productive than their Israeli peers. Nevertheless, Arab generals have published a few accounts of the Yom Kippur War from their points of view. Mohamed el Gamasy describes his experience in the war in *The October War*, as do Saad el Shazly in *The Crossing of the Suez* and Hassan el Badri and co-authors in *The Ramadan War*.[22] Naturally enough, all of these volumes concentrate heavily on the Egyptian army's undeniably well-executed crossing of the Suez Canal upon the outbreak of hostilities. All then go on to "explain" why Egypt eventually lost the war. Three books by non-Arab authors that nevertheless chronicle the war from the Arab perspective are worth mentioning here, too. In *Return to the Sinai*, Indian general D. K. Palit examines the Arab attack, with particular emphasis on Egyptian moves on the Sinai front.[23] Dani Asher, an A'MAN officer during the war, analyzes the Egyptian army's operations and tactics in *The Egyptian Strategy for the Yom Kippur War*.[24] He pays particular attention not only to the Egyptian army's innovative plan to cross the Suez Canal, but also to its novel use of antiaircraft and antitank weapons. And Kenneth Pollack's *Arabs at War* takes an in-depth look at both Syrian and Egyptian operations and tactics during the Yom Kippur War.[25]

Foreign—that is, non-Israeli and non-Arab—observers were quick to add their voices to postmortems of the war. A group of reporters from the prestigious *London Sunday Times* cobbled together a competent "instant" history of the Yom Kippur War from both sides of the line in *The Yom Kippur War*.[26] British military historian Edgar O'Ballance's volume is mainly concerned with the operational- and tactical-level moves carried out by the Syrians, Egyptians, and Israelis, tracing the movements of individual battalions, brigades, and divisions, in *No Victor, No Vanquished*.[27] The noted American military historian Trevor Dupuy provides a thorough account of the Yom Kippur War in *Elusive Victory*.[28] Anthony Cordesman and Abraham Wagner, in *The Lessons of Modern War*, examine specific dimensions of the war, such as the employment and effects of airpower and armor, in considerable detail.[29] Though neither of these last two volumes concentrates exclusively on the Yom Kippur War, both of them furnish much in the way of technical data culled from Arab, Israeli, and American sources.

A second wave of books about the hostilities emerged at the start of the present century. American military historian George Gawrych's *The Albatross of Decisive Victory* was the first of them.[30] His thesis is that, while Egypt's crushing defeat in the Six-Day War spurred it to look for ways to overcome its inferiority in air and tank warfare, Israel's spectacular victory instilled in it a sense of complacency. Consequently, the Egyptian army proved able to surprise the IDF at the outset of the Yom Kippur War, inflicting serious losses before the latter developed effective countermeasures. American journalist Howard Blum's *The Eve of Destruction* hews toward the sensational end of the spectrum, though it does contain some interesting information.[31] Israeli journalist Abraham Rabinovich's *The Yom Kippur War*, to the contrary, offers perhaps the most thorough account of the war to date.[32] It is certainly one of the most sober and readable extant. Simon Dunstan, a prolific author of popular military histories, furnishes a solid introduction to the battlefield events of the war in *The Yom Kippur War*.[33] Two important volumes that have recently become available in English are Dani Asher et al.'s *Syrians at the Border* and Emanuel Sakal's *Soldier in the Sinai*.[34] The former is an exhaustive treatment of the war on the Golan front, while the latter offers a stinging critique of the IDF's performance during the opening week of hostilities on the Sinai front from the viewpoint of an armored battalion commander. Ori Orr's *These Are My Brothers* provides an interesting personal account of the fighting on the Golan from the perspective of an armored brigade commander.[35] Though not a book per se, one more publication certainly deserves mention here. Declassified in 2012, a lengthy Central Intelligence Agency (CIA) report, titled *The 1973 Arab–Israeli War*, cogently summarizes the American assessment of the fighting, drawing on a wide range of still classified military documents to achieve this goal.[36] This report, which contains copious amounts of technical data gathered from American and Israeli military personnel, is indispensable to an appreciation of how the United States armed forces responded to the results of the war.

A few books about specific military dimensions of the Yom Kippur War are worthy of consideration. Naval special forces commander Ze'ev Almog's *Flotilla 13* tells the story of the Israel Navy (IN) special forces who prevailed in the Red Sea arena during the war, while Rabinovich's *The Boats of Cherbourg* traces the rise of the missile-armed fast patrol boat (FPB) that gave the IN a decisive advantage at sea, allowing it to dominate the Mediterranean arena during the war.[37] Israeli aviation historians Shlomo Aloni, in *Ghosts of Atonement*, and Ra'anan Weiss, in *The Israeli AF in the Yom Kippur War*, make effective use of declassified facts and figures to shed light on the air war.[38] Walter Boyne's *The Two O'Clock War*, while not offering very much in the way of commentary about the battlefield events of the war, is useful, because it supplies details about the American airlift of arms to Israel.[39] Itzhak Brook's *In the Sands of Sinai* furnishes a personal account of a doctor's experience on the battlefield.[40] Perhaps the most controversial military aspect of the war, A'MAN's failure to predict the outbreak of hostilities in early October 1973, has been examined in two books in the years since the partial opening of Israeli archives on the matter. In *The Watchman Fell Asleep*, intelligence historian Uri Bar-Joseph puts the onus squarely on the faulty thinking and complacent attitude pervasive throughout A'MAN.[41] Aryeh Shalev, the deputy director of A'MAN during the war, while not absolving military intelligence of blame in *Israel's Intelligence Assessment Before the Yom Kippur War*, also holds the political leadership accountable for the IDF's unpreparedness on the eve of the Yom Kippur War.[42]

INTRODUCTION

How This Book Fits into the Historiography of the War

Many other books about Israel, the Arab states, the Arab–Israeli conflict, superpower relations during the Cold War, and so forth, of course, review the diplomatic and/or military side(s) of the Yom Kippur War in greater or lesser detail. Moreover, when one takes into account the huge reservoir of journal, magazine, and newspaper articles, as well as think tank and government reports, the literature on the war is by now truly enormous. And, with the opening of more and more archives over the years, much more will undoubtedly be written in the future.

In light of this vast corpus of literature, one might be tempted to conclude that there really is nothing new to be said about the Yom Kippur War, at least until new facts emerge from government archives. One would be wrong, however. Some diplomatic and military issues beg for a fresh reassessment now, while others require initial treatment. In the first category, for example, the functioning of the American–Israeli relationship during the war or the influence of Israeli airpower on the battlefield are diplomatic and military issues, respectively, that would benefit from a new examination. In the second category, neither the quietly negotiated Israeli–Jordanian agreement to limit hostilities between themselves, a diplomatic issue, nor the impact of American arms transfers to Israel during the war on the outcome of hostilities, a military issue, has garnered much attention to date.

Rather than review the broad diplomatic and military strokes of the war, both of which are well covered in the extant literature, this volume is intended to address the sort of stale or neglected issues referred to above. To this end, the book is divided into three parts: the first offers reflections on a number of diplomatic issues during the war, the second on a number of military issues during the war, and the third on basic battlefield lessons derived from the war.

Part I probes three diplomatic issues. Chapter 1 examines how the all-important (for Israel) American–Israeli patron–client relationship functioned during the Yom Kippur War, maintaining that developments are best understood in light of a "security-for-autonomy" bargain between the two states. Chapter 2 traces the diplomatic efforts of Israel and Jordan to limit as much as possible the scope of a battlefield collision between them, a collision desired by neither state. And chapter 3 addresses the extent to which Israeli and American nuclear arms influenced the course of the war, concluding that their impact was essentially nonexistent.

HISTORIOGRAPHY OF THE WAR

Part II tackles three battle-related issues. Chapter 4 assesses the IDF's approach to combined arms warfare during the Yom Kippur War, asserting that critics of its performance focus too intently on the opening days of hostilities and not enough on the fighting thereafter. Chapter 5 grapples with the question of why Israel recovered from its initial shock more quickly on the Golan than in the Sinai, arguing that the combined effects of a number of variables account for the IDF's performance on each front early in the war. And chapter 6 revisits the effect of Israeli airpower on the outcome of the Yom Kippur War via a comparison with its effect on the outcome of the Six-Day War, concluding—perhaps in opposition to most informed observers—that it actually played a more crucial part in the IDF's former victory.

Part III considers some of the lessons of the war. Chapter 7 weighs the extent to which American arms transfers to Israel during the Yom Kippur War affected battlefield events, stressing that these weapons deliveries were not nearly as critical to the IDF's victory as is commonly thought. The final two chapters ponder how the American and Israeli defense establishments understood the war. Chapter 8 examines the American reaction to the battlefield events of the Yom Kippur War by unpacking the aforementioned CIA report—a report that demonstrates clearly that, in the opinion of the American military establishment, the war represented an evolution, but not a revolution, in military affairs. And chapter 9 takes a look at how the IDF rebuilt itself in the wake of the war as a result of the lessons it drew from the fighting, placing an increased emphasis on quantity and balance in its postwar order of battle.

Finally, the chapters in this volume need not be consulted in any particular order, because the book is organized thematically rather than chronologically. One caveat is in order here in this regard: overlap in content across chapters has been unavoidable, in order to ensure that each chapter is complete in itself and not dependent upon any other(s). The issues explored in this book, after all, are related in many respects and are based upon the same set of underlying facts. This decision has been taken in order to accommodate readers who may not be fully conversant with the basic facts of the Yom Kippur War, but who intend to limit their perusal of this volume to one or two issues. The author apologizes in advance to any reader who may find this repetition a bit tiresome.

Part I
Diplomacy

Diplomacy: The art of restraining power.
Henry Kissinger

1

The American–Israeli Relationship

The relationship between the United States and Israel is frequently called an alliance. This label has been applied in analyses of both alliance systems in general and the American–Israeli partnership in particular.¹ The term "alliance," of course, has been defined in different ways by observers of international politics over the years; however, most of them would agree that an alliance is a formal agreement "between [or among] sovereign states for the putative purpose of coordinating their behavior in the event of specified contingencies of a military nature."² Each state in an alliance, in other words, is bound to every other state in that alliance through a web of contractual entitlements and obligations.

The relationship between the United States and Israel has never constituted an alliance, because neither side has ever been bound to the other through a formal agreement, such as the one that ties together members of the North Atlantic Treaty Organization (NATO). Rather, since the 1960s, when it began in earnest, the American–Israeli partnership has been an informal one between a patron, the United States, and a client, Israel. The difference between an alliance and a patron–client relationship is not simply semantic (formal versus informal), as the potential costs and benefits associated with each arrangement are not the same. The United States and Israel have deliberately opted for a patron–client relationship, because each state thinks that its national interests are better served by an arrangement in which it has no formal obligations to the other state. The United States has favored this sort of relationship primarily because it has not wanted to be too closely identified with Israel, while Israel has favored this sort of relationship primarily because it has not wanted to be under the American thumb in a contractual sense.

At the heart of this patron–client relationship has been what may be termed a "security-for-autonomy" bargain. Israel, as the weaker state in the relationship, has informally ceded a measure of its freedom to pursue its own foreign policy to the United States, the stronger state in the relationship, in exchange for vital military, diplomatic, and economic assistance. The United States, on the other hand, has informally extended this assistance in order to enhance its ability to pursue its national interests in the Middle East.[3]

The Road to the War

The American–Israeli patron–client relationship experienced a period of unusual tranquility from the end of the 1969–70 War of Attrition until the outbreak of the 1973 Yom Kippur War, principally because, in American eyes, the Arab–Israeli conflict took a back seat to radical Arab and Soviet troublemaking in the Middle East during these years. The United States even began to regard Israel as a "strategic asset" that, under certain circumstances, could serve as a bulwark against radical Arab and Soviet expansionism in the region, especially after the Israel Defense Forces (IDF) had assisted in the survival of Jordan's pro-Western regime in the September 1970 Jordanian civil war by intimidating Syria into curbing its support of the Palestine Liberation Organization (PLO), which unsuccessfully sought to topple the Jordanian government through an armed insurrection. Consequently, the United States transferred significant quantities of arms to Israel without attaching any real strings during these years. This rosy (for Israel) situation would come to an abrupt halt with the outbreak of the Yom Kippur War.

"No war, no peace" aptly summarized the condition of the Arab–Israeli conflict after the War of Attrition. The Arab world rejected the postwar status quo, which found Israel still in complete control of the territories that it had captured in the 1967 Six-Day War. Unable to wrest these lands away by force, the Arab world remained unwilling to pay the price—peace treaties with Israel—that would have been necessary to recover them peacefully. Israel, to the contrary, approved of the postwar status quo, and therefore showed little inclination to part with territory in exchange for anything less than peace treaties with its neighbors. All diplomatic efforts to break this stalemate, including a major push in 1971, came to naught.

Consequently, Egypt and Syria concluded that another round of full-scale warfare would be necessary for them to achieve a resolution to the Arab–Israeli conflict consistent with their national interests. These states believed that, if their armies could inflict heavy losses on the IDF, seize and hold pieces of the Sinai and Golan, respectively, and involve the United States and the Soviet Union in the fighting, then they could fulfill their strategic aims, even if they were ultimately to suffer defeat on the battlefield.

But Egypt and Syria still required the military means to implement their design. They recognized that they would neither be able to exact a significant toll in men and machines nor capture territory unless they could counter the IDF's overwhelming tank and air superiority. Massive Soviet arms transfers in the form of the most modern antitank and antiaircraft weapons systems available at the time, however, gave them these means. By the fall of 1973, then, Egypt and Syria had a viable war option.

Despite the fact that Israel's military and civilian intelligence services had gathered copious amounts of high-quality data about Arab arms acquisitions, operational plans, troop movements, and so forth, both the IDF and the Israeli government remained convinced until the day war actually erupted that Israel did not face an imminent prospect of hostilities.[4] The problem lay not in the realm of information gathering, but rather in the sphere of information processing and governmental decision making.

The Arab world, especially Egypt, had spoken on more than one occasion in the early 1970s about engaging in war "to restore Arab rights," but had not acted on its words. Rhetoric of this sort unaccompanied by any action served to lull both the IDF and Israeli government into a sense of complacency. The Arab world, they believed, would not challenge Israel on the battlefield so long as the latter remained the strongest power in the region. They did not conceive of the notion that the Arab world might be willing to endure a military setback in order to achieve a diplomatic triumph.

The Patron–Client Relationship in the War

Blinded by this set of assumptions, collectively known as "the concept," both the IDF and Israeli government misinterpreted fresh information in the days before the outbreak of war that pointed clearly in the direction of hostilities. When Egypt and Syria mobilized their armies and deployed them along the cease-fire lines in the Sinai and on the Golan, Israel considered this development to be nothing more than routine military exercises or, perhaps, saber rattling (in response to a humiliating air defeat in mid-September in which 13 Syrian fighter-bombers had been shot down in a dogfight). And, when Soviet citizens departed Egypt in large numbers, Israel chalked this development up to a feud between the Soviet Union and its client.

Only at the last moment, literally hours before the beginning of the Arab offensives, when they received irrefutable proof of Egyptian and Syrian intentions from an unimpeachable source, did the IDF and the Israeli government acknowledge their terrible mistake. Nevertheless, Israel still had sufficient time to prepare and execute a preemptive air strike at the outset of the Yom Kippur War.[5] IDF general headquarters (GHQ) sought immediate authorization for a preemptive strike, arguing that, though it might not be as devastating as Israel's opening attack during the Six-Day War, such a strike would put an unready IDF, which needed a minimum of 24–48 hours to mobilize and deploy its reserve forces, the core of its combat power, in a far better position to withstand the initial Arab onslaughts.

The Israeli government, though, refused to sanction a preemptive attack, a decision that President Richard Nixon's administration, particularly in the person of Secretary of State Henry Kissinger, encouraged in an emphatic manner.[6] Prime Minister Golda Meir herself remarked via a letter that:

> You know the reasons why we took no preemptive action. Our failure to take such action is the reason for our situation now. If I had given the chief of staff authority to preempt, as he had recommended, some hours before the attack began, there is no doubt that our situation would now be different.[7]

Indeed, the secretary of state had long cautioned Israel against a preemptive strike in conversations with Israeli officials. Simcha Dinitz, Israeli Ambassador to the United States, remarked that, "Dr. Kissinger had always told me, whatever happens, [do not] be the one that strikes first. He told this to [former Israeli Ambassador Yitzhak] Rabin too."[8] And, on October 6, the day the war began, Kissinger sent a cable to Nixon saying that:

> We are urgently communicating with the Israelis, warning them against any preemptive action. . . . I then called Israeli Chargé [Mordechai] Shalev [and] I emphasized to him the essentiality of restraint on the Israeli part, and said there must be no preemptive strike. . . . Shalev called back shortly thereafter and said his government assured us there would be no preemptive action. Shortly thereafter we received a message from Prime Minister Meir confirming this.[9]

Caught between IDF GHQ and the United States administration, the Israeli government chose to follow the position of Israel's patron rather than the advice of its own military command.

Instead of potentially wresting the initiative away from the Egyptian and Syrian armies, consequently, the IDF had to absorb the first blow, resulting in serious reverses during the early days of the fighting. Not only did it suffer heavy losses among men and machines, but it also gave ground in the Sinai and on the Golan. By the second day of the war, the IDF appeared to be in dire straits on both fronts.

From the moment the war broke out, Israel asked the United States to provide arms. In the same meeting in which Shalev had delivered Meir's letter to Kissinger, he presented a second message:

> The Prime Minister requests that the equipment urgently requested of the United States Government be supplied. This is especially important because of the quantitative superiority of the enemy, and because we have been forced to adopt a defensive strategy.[10]

Israel had already put in requests for tanks, fighter-bombers, various types of ammunition and electronic systems, and other items.

While the United States approved, albeit rather grudgingly, the dispatch of small amounts of arms to be carried in Israeli cargo aircraft within a couple of days, it dragged its feet on the issue of a large-scale American supply effort.[11] The Nixon administration consented to the supply of some "consumables," such as air-to-air missiles, tank and artillery ammunition, electronic systems, and so forth; however, it balked at the supply of "hardware," such as tanks and fighter-bombers, items that could not be concealed from Arab eyes. Moreover, discord between the State and Defense Departments held up even this trickle of arms. During the first week of the war, therefore, the only American arms that reached Israel consisted of those consumables that could be loaded onto a handful of Israeli cargo flights.[12]

The American policy of deflecting the Israeli government's arms requests ended abruptly on October 13, when Nixon personally authorized a massive airlift—later augmented by a sealift—of arms to Israel. On October 14, the first American cargo aircraft arrived in Israel. Almost a week had gone by since a similar Soviet airlift of arms to its Arab clients had got underway. The Nixon administration approved the airlift only after it became clear that Egypt and its Soviet patron had rejected an American attempt to arrange a cease-fire. Kissinger put it thusly:

CHAPTER 1

> We [the United States] did not put [any arms] into the Middle East [during the first week of the war], except to permit El Al [i.e., Israeli cargo flights] to pick up I think six planeloads of stuff here that was carried in converted [aircraft], and was very minor. The Soviets put in 284 planeloads [of arms during the first week], amounting to 4,000 tons. And moreover, they dragged their feet on negotiations to bring about a cease-fire.... So we felt we had no alternative except to start an airlift of our own...[13]

The American resupply effort would easily outpace the Soviet resupply effort, a development that undoubtedly contributed to the eventual Arab decision to seek a cease-fire.

Though American arms were not forthcoming at the start of the Yom Kippur War, the IDF nevertheless quickly recovered from its initial reverses. Its qualitative superiority vis-à-vis its Arab opponents soon manifested itself on the northern and southern battlefields. On the Golan, the IDF smashed the Syrian army and drove it from Israeli-controlled territory by October 10. The IDF then advanced into Syria, seizing a sizable chunk of territory, which brought its artillery within range of the Syrian capital of Damascus no later than October 14, before the first American cargo aircraft had even landed on Israeli soil. In the Sinai, the IDF halted the Egyptian offensive across the Suez Canal, defeating a major tank thrust toward the peninsula's mountain passes on October 14. The IDF then counterattacked across the canal into Egypt proper beginning on October 15—that is, before American arms started to reach its forces in meaningful quantities (though the promise of those arms may have affected to some degree the pace, scope, and intensity of the Israeli counteroffensive).

Once the IDF crossed the Suez Canal into Egypt proper, the Yom Kippur War moved into its final stage. In contrast to the opening week of the war, Egypt now actively sought an end to the fighting, in order to avert the total collapse of its army, as the IDF steadily advanced toward the Egyptian capital of Cairo. IDF forces would eventually finish the war a mere 100 kilometers from the city. Consequently, the United States and the Soviet Union worked to hammer out a durable cease-fire; however, several attempts to stop the hostilities proved abortive, as both the Egyptian army and the IDF continued to fight in order to improve their respective military positions.

The IDF took advantage of Egyptian cease-fire violations to move steadily deeper into Egypt, eventually surrounding the Egyptian Third Army. The Nixon administration quietly approved of the IDF's advances in the face of Egyptian violations.[14] But it would not countenance the destruction of the Third Army itself.[15] Despite getting into something of a nuclear showdown with the Soviet Union, as both superpowers sought to back their clients in public, the United States placed great pressure on Israel to spare the Egyptian Third army. Kissinger issued the following blunt warning to the Israeli government:

> First, he [Nixon] wanted to make it absolutely clear that we cannot permit the destruction of the Egyptian [Third] army under conditions achieved after a cease-fire was reached in part by negotiations in which we participated. Therefore it is an option that does not exist. . . . Secondly, he would like from you . . . an answer to the question of non-military supplies permitted to reach the army. If you cannot agree to that, we will have to support in the [United Nations (UN)] a resolution that will deal with enforcement [of earlier UN resolutions]. We have been driven to this reluctantly by your inability to reach a decision. . . . You will not be permitted to destroy this army.[16]

The American administration even suggested to the Israeli government at one point that the United States would stand aside while the Soviet army joined the fighting to save the Third Army.[17]

Israeli Foreign Minister Abba Eban phrased his country's dilemma this way:

> Should we attempt the destruction of Egypt's Third Army at the risk of Soviet intervention, or should we ensure American support . . . by allowing the Third Army to be saved?[18]

After some difficult haggling with the American administration over the precise terms of a cease-fire agreement, the Israeli government ultimately chose to loosen the IDF's grip on the Third Army, thereby reducing the magnitude of Israel's victory in the Yom Kippur War.

Disagreement between the United States and Israel did not come to an end when the guns fell silent. During postwar disengagement negotiations, the Nixon and, later, Ford administrations placed considerable pressure on the Israeli government to make concessions to Egypt and Syria, especially in the form of withdrawals from portions of the Sinai and Golan, respectively.[19] To get Israel to make the desired concessions, the United States once again used a carrot-and-stick approach.

On the one hand, the Nixon and Ford administrations promised to bolster the American–Israeli relationship, including the arms pipeline,

CHAPTER 1

If the Israeli government were to give back chunks of the Sinai and Golan. On the other hand, implicitly at times and explicitly at others, the United States threatened to punish Israel, holding out the possibility of a disruption in assistance, particularly arms transfers, if the Israeli government were to reject American demands. Indeed, the Ford administration even initiated a "reassessment" of the entire American–Israeli relationship, implying that the United States could drastically reduce its military, economic, and diplomatic support of Israel if the Israeli government did not satisfy American wishes.

For its part, Israel resisted American pressure for as long as it could do so without actually harming the bilateral relationship; however, in the end, it gave in to American demands. It eventually withdrew from a large portion of the Sinai and a small part of the Golan in exchange for increased American backing.

Analysis of American and Israeli Conduct in the War

The conduct of the United States in the Yom Kippur War grew out of the same set of national interests that had driven American policy during the Six-Day War and the War of Attrition. First, the United States sought to contain radical Arab and Soviet influence in the Middle East, primarily in order to protect pro-Western Arab states and their oil resources. Second, the United States did not want to get into a conflict in the region, because its armed forces still remained bogged down in Vietnam. Furthermore, a military confrontation with the Arab world or the Soviet Union could lead to the direst consequences for the United States, including the possibility of a full-scale war between the superpowers. And, third, the United States sought to make sure that Israel's basic security was not put in jeopardy.

In contrast to the Six-Day War and the War of Attrition, however, when the United States sought merely to prevent a deterioration in the regional status quo, the Nixon administration spied a golden opportunity near the end of the Yom Kippur War to alter the status quo to American advantage. Both Nixon and Kissinger concluded that the United States could significantly roll back Soviet influence—and greatly expand American influence—in the Middle East, particularly in Egypt, if the administration played its cards right at the end of the war.

A regional realignment, though, would not occur if Israel were to win an overwhelming military victory like it had in the Six-Day War. The Nixon administration, therefore, wanted to engineer a battlefield stalemate, particularly between Israel and Egypt, in order to promote postwar negotiations, which the United States would then mediate to its own benefit. Nixon's words plainly reveal the administration's intention:

> I believed that only a battlefield stalemate would provide the foundation in which fruitful negotiations might begin: Any equilibrium—even if only an equilibrium of mutual exhaustion—would make it easier to reach an enforceable settlement. Therefore, I was convinced that we must not use our influence to bring about a cease-fire that would leave the parties in such imbalance that negotiations for a permanent settlement would never begin.[20]

Israel's dependence on American arms would be manipulated by the administration in an attempt to achieve this objective.

Before the shooting began, the United States firmly believed that the IDF would swiftly crush its Arab opponents on the battlefield. Hence, the Nixon administration strongly discouraged an Israeli preemptive attack, implying that Israel should not expect to receive so much as a bullet from the United States if it opened hostilities, because such a strike, it thought, would only add to the IDF's ability to smash its Arab foes. The same thinking led the United States to drag its feet for over a week in dispatching arms to Israel. Not until after it had become evident that the IDF had suffered some early reverses on the battlefield, not until after a massive Soviet airlift had been under way for days, and not until after Egypt had rejected the notion of a cease-fire did the United States authorize a matching airlift to Israel. Kissinger summarized the American position as follows:

> We pursued this [a cease-fire] until Saturday of the first week—that is to say until 13 October. On 13 October it was clear that the Soviets could not deliver the Egyptians to what was in effect a cease-fire in place, and to which we had obtained Israeli acquiescence, more or less. When that occurred we felt we had no choice except to go another route.... And this is the reason why we started the airlift.... It is the principal reason why we started the airlift...[21]

The United States, to put it another way, only began an airlift once its first attempt to engineer a battlefield stalemate had wrecked itself on the shoals of Egyptian and Soviet intransigence, leaving Israel at a potential military disadvantage in the face of continuing Soviet arms shipments to the Arab world.

Egypt's refusal to agree to a cease-fire early in the war meant that the Nixon administration could not in the end bring about the battlefield stalemate that it envisioned originally; however, the United States could still limit the scope of the Israeli triumph in the war by using arms deliveries to gain leverage over Israel. Nixon himself made this very point in both harsh and more temperate language on at least a couple of occasions:

> [We have] got to squeeze the Israelis. . . . [We have] got to squeeze them [very] hard. And [that is] the way it is going to be done.[22]

> In order to have the influence we need to bring Israel to a settlement, we have to have their [sic] confidence. That is why [the] airlift. . . . [W]e have to do enough to have a bargaining position to bring Israel kicking and screaming to the table.[23]

Thus, the United States permitted Israel to surround the Egyptian Third Army (in order to improve America's bargaining position vis-à-vis Egypt and the Soviet Union), but it would not allow the IDF to destroy this army (in order to acquire Egyptian favor). The Nixon administration, in short, spared Arab "honor," making it possible for the United States to mediate postwar negotiations without meaningful Soviet participation. This diplomatic agenda also accounts for the administration's carrot-and-stick approach to Israel during postwar negotiations.

Israel's conduct in the Yom Kippur War is not comprehensible unless it is examined in the context of the American–Israeli patron–client relationship. Unquestionably, the Israeli government's fear of a negative American reaction constituted the decisive reason why it dismissed the IDF's advice to launch a preemptive attack. The Israeli government believed that, if the IDF struck the initial blow, the United States would not assist Israel during the war.[24] Defense Minister Moshe Dayan summed up his government's attitude:

> [I]f American help was to be sought, then the United States had to be given full proof that it was not we [the Israelis] who desired war—even if this ruled out preemptive action and handicapped us in the military campaign.[25]

Had the Israeli government been certain of American support in the wake of a preemptive strike, it would almost certainly have consented to such an attack; however, faced with a powerful Arab war coalition that had the unshakeable support of the Soviet Union, Israel simply could not risk the loss of American goodwill.

Likewise, Israel's dependence on American arms convinced the Israeli government to accept, albeit tentatively, a Nixon administration cease-fire proposal during the first week of the war. Similarly, the administration's threat to abandon Israel compelled the Israeli government to loosen the IDF's grip on the Egyptian Third Army later in the war. Indeed, in order to explain this decision, Meir herself made explicit reference to the American–Israeli relationship:

> There is only one country to which we can turn and sometimes we have to give in to it—even when we know we shouldn't. But it is the only real friend we have, and a very powerful one. We [do not] have to say yes to everything, but [let us] call things by their proper name. There is nothing to be ashamed of when a small country like Israel, in this situation, has to give in sometimes to the United States. And when we do say yes, [let us] for God's sake not pretend that it is otherwise. . . .[26]

Finally, the Israeli government felt that, in the aftermath of a very destructive war, one in which its internal capabilities had been heavily drained by the fighting, it had no alternative but to trade the postwar concessions desired by the United States for continued American support, particularly in the area of arms acquisitions. A firm American–Israeli patron–client relationship, the Israeli government reasoned, took precedence over the retention of chunks of the Sinai and Golan in regard to its national interests.

Summary

If the United States and Israel had been enmeshed in an alliance during the Yom Kippur War, the obvious discord between them during the three weeks of fighting would have been either entirely absent or, at least, quite muted. Each country, presumably, would have fulfilled its obligations toward the other under the terms of the alliance without the need to haggle over every item of mutual concern. The difficult—even acrimonious at times—relationship between the United States and Israel stemmed precisely from the fact that they were in a patron–client relationship. The lack of obligations to each other left each country free to attempt to manipulate the relationship to its particular advantage. The United States sought to influence Israeli policy in order to achieve America's diplomatic objectives, while Israel sought to acquire arms from the United States in order to secure its military objectives. Here, the security-for-autonomy bargain at the heart of the relationship came into play. The arms that the United States furnished to Israel bolstered the latter's security, albeit mostly in the aftermath of the war. In exchange for these arms, Israel surrendered a measure of its freedom of action to the United States so that the latter could pursue its perceived national interests in the Middle East and beyond.

2

The Israeli–Jordanian Relationship

During both the 1967 Six-Day War and the 1973 Yom Kippur War, the Jordanian government faced strong domestic and foreign pressure to unleash its armed forces against Israel. King Hussein's subjects, especially the very sizable Palestinian community, sought nothing less than the disappearance of Israel from the map. Hussein could not afford to dismiss entirely the view of the masses, as their volatility represented a chronic threat to his reign. And, in the eyes of the Arab world, he risked being seen as a traitor to the Arab cause if he did not join Egypt, Syria, and Iraq in their war against Israel, a development with the potential to place his throne in jeopardy.

Yet Jordan behaved quite differently in the two wars. In the events leading up to the Six-Day War, the Jordanian government adopted an openly belligerent stance. It joined with Egypt and Syria in a war pact against Israel, and it put its armed forces under Egyptian command.[1] Once the fighting between Israel and Egypt got underway, the Jordanian government ignored the Israeli government's entreaties, delivered via the United Nations (UN), to the effect that Israel had no desire to engage in battle with Jordan, and that it would not do so unless fired upon first. King Hussein's decision to open a second front against Israel in spite of this offer of nonaggression not only cost him his air force, as well as much of his tank and artillery strength, but also all of Jordanian territory west of the Jordan River—that is, all of Judea and Samaria.

During the Yom Kippur War, to the contrary, Jordan did not participate in either the planning or execution of the initial Egyptian–Syrian surprise attack against Israel.[2] Nor did it open up a third front against Israel in the Jordan Valley. The bridges spanning the Jordan River continued to carry civilian traffic between the two banks, as they did during peacetime.[3] Not until the second week of the war did the Jordanian government dispatch forces to fight on behalf of the Arab

CHAPTER 2

cause—and then only one tank brigade to the Golan that later reluctantly took part in two abortive Syrian–Iraqi attacks on Israeli positions in the southern part of the region, both of them easily repulsed by the Israel Defense Forces (IDF).

Though the Jordanian armed forces in the fall of 1973 possessed a modest order of battle by Middle Eastern standards, Jordan still had enough military resources and the tactical skill to at least attempt a crossing of the Jordan River with tank forces. Furthermore, Amman commanded the resources necessary to mount air strikes and artillery barrages against Israel from the east bank of the river. Alternatively, the Jordanian government possessed the military resources necessary to dispatch additional brigades to fight alongside Syrian forces on the Golan—and all of them at an earlier stage in the war. Had the Jordanians either opened up a third front in the Jordan Valley or moved resolutely to assist the Syrian attack at the outset of hostilities, the IDF might not have been able to halt one—perhaps both—of the initial Syrian and Egyptian offensives. Even without Jordanian participation during the early days of the fighting, after all, an unprepared IDF just barely prevented Syrian and Egyptian breakthroughs on the Golan and in the Sinai, respectively.

For its part, Israel never evinced much concern about the prospect of a third front in the Jordan Valley. Aside from mining some of the major roadways in Judea and Samaria, the IDF apparently took no special precautions here, nor did it siphon off significant forces from either the Golan or Sinai front to reinforce its positions in Judea and Samaria.[4] Likewise, Israel never displayed intense concern that Jordan would participate heavily in the fighting on the Golan, and the IDF did not reinforce its positions here after the deployment of the Jordanian tank brigade.

Why did Israel respond rather nonchalantly to the prospect of Jordan intervening in the war in a consequential way? Part of the explanation lies in deterrence. Prime Minister Golda Meir's government reasoned that the Jordanian government—knowing full well that the Israel Air Force (IAF) could pulverize not only Jordan's military forces, but also the kingdom's infrastructure—would not be so reckless as to antagonize Israel by opening up a third front in the Jordan Valley or by engaging wholeheartedly in the Syrian offensive on the Golan. The rest of the explanation is to be found in the fact that Israel and Jordan quietly cooperated during the war to limit hostilities between them.

That Israel and Jordan were "friendly enemies" by the outbreak of the Yom Kippur War is certainly not a revelation. Israel had already helped Hussein's regime to survive a combined Palestine Liberation

Organization (PLO)–Syrian attack in the summer of 1970.[5] IDF air and ground maneuvers in full view of Syria, combined with public warnings from Israeli officials, convinced Damascus to restrain the extent of its intervention on behalf of the PLO in the latter's effort to overthrow the king's regime, permitting the Jordanian armed forces to eject both Palestinian and Syrian units from the kingdom. Indeed, Egypt and Syria deliberately kept Jordan in the dark about their surprise attack on Israel in October 1973, because they did not trust the latter to keep its mouth shut, so to speak.

Nevertheless, even if Israeli–Jordanian cooperation during the Yom Kippur War is no real surprise in itself, recently released United States government documents shed light on its modus operandi during the fighting. The present chapter is intended to chronicle this cooperation; however, two caveats must be kept firmly in mind. First, it is almost certain that some American documents that bear on the issue (e.g., documents in Central Intelligence Agency (CIA) and National Security Agency (NSA) archives) have not been declassified yet. Second, and equally important, Israeli and Jordanian documents relevant to the issue—which are not available for public scrutiny yet—have not, of course, been consulted here, either. Collectively speaking, these American, Israeli, and Jordanian documents would undoubtedly add much to an understanding of the cooperation between Israel and Jordan during the war. The present chapter, then, represents nothing more than a tentative first stab at reconstructing Israeli–Jordanian cooperation in the conflict.

Before the Yom Kippur War

Israeli and Jordanian leaders met face-to-face on no less than four occasions in the months before the Yom Kippur War.[6] In the late fall of 1972 or the early winter of 1973, Prime Minister Golda Meir and the king discussed the possibility of achieving an Israeli–Jordanian peace agreement. In the early spring and early summer of 1973, they spoke twice about the Arab–Israeli conflict in general terms, as well as the potential for renewed Arab–Israeli hostilities. The tone of these meetings seemed to be relaxed. The fourth meeting occurred in early autumn, less than two weeks prior to the outbreak of war, and it had a somewhat more urgent tone.[7] Hussein informed Meir that, in Jordan's opinion, Egypt and Syria might be preparing to embark on a coordinated war against Israel. The Meir government and the IDF, however, dismissed Hussein's concerns for two reasons: (1) their own intelli-

CHAPTER 2

gence assessment determined that war remained a low probability event (i.e., until the last hours before fighting actually broke out) and (2) the king had not provided concrete information about an imminent attack, only vague conjecture based on knowledge of Syria's military buildup on the Golan.

From Nonbelligerence to Damage Control

The Yom Kippur War erupted in the mid-afternoon of October 6, and it dragged on until October 24, when a more or less stable cease-fire agreement finally took hold on both fronts. For the purpose of tracing Israeli–Jordanian cooperation during the fighting, the war is best divided into two distinct phases: the first week, from October 6–12, when Jordan refrained from taking an active part in hostilities, and the following two weeks, from October 13–24, when the Jordanian armed forces participated in several attacks on the IDF in conjunction with its Syrian and Iraqi "allies."

From day one of the war, Jordan came under intense pressure to engage Israel in battle. Interestingly, the initial pressure did not come primarily from Egypt and Syria. So long as they perceived themselves to be making progress on the battlefield, they felt no special urgency in seeking Jordan's assistance. Rather, other Arab states were more insistent at first. No later than October 8, for example, King Faisal, the Saudi Arabian monarch, demanded that Jordan not only join the war, but also that it allow those of the kingdom's troops then stationed on Jordanian soil to depart for the Golan.[8] On October 9, a Soviet envoy met with Hussein in an effort to cajole Jordan into entering the fray.[9] Only after the tide began to turn against them did Egypt and Syria start to put real pressure on the king to dispatch Jordanian forces to the battlefield. By October 10, Egypt's President Anwar Sadat sent a message to Hussein urging that he either allow PLO irregulars to resume attacks on Israel from Jordan or deploy Jordanian forces to the Golan.[10] And, by this date, Syria's President Hafez Assad asked Jordan to send an armored division to the Golan.[11]

Israel and the United States, to the contrary, put pressure on Jordan to stay out of the war. To make certain that Jordan did not "make waves"—that is, did not open a third front or dispatch large forces to the Golan—Israeli military officers and cabinet ministers made "well-rehearsed" threats to their American interlocutors in the early days of the war to the effect that the IDF would crush Jordan if it dared to take on Israel, knowing full well that these threats would be communicated to Jordan via American channels.¹² Israel was also in direct contact with Jordan during the war, so it is safe to assume that the Meir government placed direct pressure on Hussein's government to keep Jordan out of the fighting, though probably in somewhat more circumspect and delicate language than it employed in conversations with American officials.¹³ For its part, the United States not only relayed Israel's threats to Jordan, but also added its own voice in support of Jordanian restraint.¹⁴ Hussein's American interlocutors impressed upon him the grim mood in Israel, and they urged him not to do the bidding of his Arab rivals and the Soviet Union.

Jordan considered itself to be caught between a rock and a hard place. On the one hand, Jordanian officials perceived that the potential costs of fighting Israel far outweighed the potential benefits. But, on the other hand, Jordan could not stand aloof, especially if the war went badly for Egypt and Syria, and especially if other Arab states, such as Iraq and Saudi Arabia, sent their troops into battle. To stand aside at such an hour would be to court disaster for the regime, as Hussein would be branded a traitor at home and abroad.

The king's first inclination, therefore, was to plead with the United States to arrange as quickly as possible a cease-fire, which would then be followed by negotiations leading to a comprehensive settlement of the Arab–Israeli conflict.¹⁵ Concomitantly, Hussein stalled on Arab and Soviet requests to deploy his own troops to the Golan, refused to permit Saudi Arabian troops in Jordan to leave for the area, refused to aid Iraqi forces in their movement to the Golan front, and turned down Egypt's request to allow his country to be used as a base by PLO irregulars.¹⁶ And, though he complained to the United States about repeated "violations" of Jordanian airspace—Israeli aircraft sometimes flew over the kingdom's territory on their way to attack targets in Syria—Jordan took no measures to impede these overflights.¹⁷ Finally, Jordan firmly rejected the idea of opening a third front against Israel.¹⁸

By October 10, with no cease-fire agreement in sight and with the war now going very badly for Syria, however, Hussein despairingly concluded that Jordan could no longer afford to be seen to do nothing in support of the Arab cause. In addition to a general mobilization of the Jordanian armed forces, the king told his American interlocutors that he had no choice but to dispatch a tank brigade to the Golan. He added that he hoped that this deployment could be coordinated with Israel, so that the IDF and Jordanian armed forces would not come to blows. The idea was to send the tank brigade to a quiet sector on the southern Golan, where it would relieve Syrian troops for redeployment to the battlefield.¹⁹

CHAPTER 2

Once Hussein decided to move a tank brigade into Syria, he communicated his reasoning and intention to Israel. He did so indirectly, through American and, especially, British channels, as well as directly, via a lengthy written memo addressed and delivered to Meir herself. For its part, the Meir government naturally refused to give the king a blanket guarantee that the IDF would not engage the Jordanian tank brigade, but also made it very clear that Israel was not interested in a fight with Jordan if the latter's forces did not advance onto the battlefield.[20] With this quiet agreement in hand, Jordanian forces reached the Jordan–Syria frontier on the night of October 12–13, and at least part of the tank brigade was inside Syrian territory no later than October 13.[21]

The second phase of Israeli–Jordanian cooperation—what might best be termed the "damage limitation" phase—now got underway. Within days of the Jordanian deployment, Hussein informed the Meir government that Syria had begun to put tremendous pressure on Jordan either to fight or to withdraw its forces back to Jordanian territory. The king added that he now had no choice but to commit his troops against Israel, under the auspices of the Iraqi expeditionary force. The Meir government responded that the IDF would defend itself, but it also hoped that the confrontation with the Jordanian tank brigade could be limited, urging Jordan not to engage heavily in battle and not to augment its existing deployment in Syria.[22]

In the event, Jordanian forces participated in two Syrian–Iraqi assaults on Israeli positions, on October 16 and 19, as well as in some minor skirmishes on other days.[23] The Jordanians possessed the most skilled of all Arab military forces engaged in the Yom Kippur War, but their troops nevertheless turned out to be no match for the IDF, particularly when attacking into the teeth of stout Israeli defenses. In the course of these two engagements, the IDF destroyed a few dozen Jordanian tanks and armored personnel carriers (APCs), apparently at scant cost to itself. The Jordanian effort was not helped by the utter disorganization of the Syrian–Iraqi assaults, which saw Jordan's forces mistakenly fired upon by Syrian and Iraqi troops, adding to the former's losses and drawing the scorn of the king.[24]

On October 21, after the Golan front had quieted down considerably, Hussein sent elements of a second tank brigade to the area, principally in order to be able to claim at home and abroad that he had sent substantial forces to assist the Arab cause before a cease-fire agreement came into effect.[25] At their peak, the Jordanian forces in Syria had 180 tanks, 120 APCs, and 40 artillery tubes.[26] Concomitantly, the king told his American interlocutors that, while Jordan would commit itself to the cease-fire agreement then under discussion by the United States and the Soviet Union, and while Jordanian forces would not allow Iraqi units to move through their positions to attack the IDF, he would have no choice but to allow his troops to participate in a renewed offensive against Israel if Syria rejected an end to hostilities, as they were under Syrian command.[27] This scenario, however, did not materialize in the event, as Syria ultimately decided to observe the call for a cease-fire.

Summary

Though Israel and Jordan did come to blows in the Yom Kippur War, the timing, scope, duration, and intensity of these encounters were such that neither side suffered crippling losses. Militarily speaking, Israel had been spared the nightmare of fighting on three fronts simultaneously, and it had been given the opportunity to stabilize the Golan and Sinai fronts before Jordanian troops entered the fray, while Jordan had preserved its armed forces largely intact, an important consideration for a state that relied very heavily on them to keep the regime in power. Diplomatically speaking, Israel had avoided a situation in which it would have been compelled to threaten the very survival of a regime that routinely conducted itself as a tacit partner against Palestinian and radical Arab adventurism, while Jordan had maintained its quiet relationship with Israel without alienating its own populace or the rest of the Arab world. The fact that Jordanian forces had engaged in battle with the IDF—and that at least a few Jordanian troops had become "martyrs" (i.e., had been killed in battle)—spared Hussein the consequences of being labeled a traitor to the Arab cause at home and abroad. Even though the Arab League would later recognize the PLO as the "sole legitimate representative" of the Palestinian people against the king's will, the legitimacy of his own regime was not seriously questioned by his Arab "brothers." Both Israel and Jordan, in short, reaped significant benefits from their wartime cooperation.

3

Nuclear Arms, Deterrence, and Compellence

Though Israel has never formally admitted to the possession of nuclear arms, informed observers contend that the country has had a nuclear option for a number of decades now. The date on which Israel actually crossed the nuclear weapons threshold remains unknown with any certainty. The leading historian of the country's nuclear arms program believes that Israel assembled its first bombs on the eve of the 1967 Six-Day War.[1] Not all observers may agree with this particular assessment, but most of them would concur that Israel had the capacity to produce nuclear weapons before the 1973 Yom Kippur War.

Israel, of course, did not employ nuclear arms in this war. Nor did it publicly threaten to employ them. Nevertheless, some observers maintain that the country's nuclear arsenal had a significant impact on how the war unfolded. Two distinct lines of thought exist with respect to this conclusion. The first insists that Israel's nuclear arsenal affected Arab conduct, while the second claims that it influenced American conduct. Neither of these two lines of thought, however, offers compelling evidence or argumentation on behalf of its assertion, as will become clear after a very brief detour into the history of Israel's nuclear weapons program and its role in shaping the American–Israeli patron–client relationship.

Nuclear Arms and the American–Israeli Relationship

Israel's nuclear arms program is almost as old as the state itself.[2] Heavily outnumbered in fighting men and machines by its Arab foes, deprived of strategic depth and defensible borders, and with no formal allies to come to its assistance in a time of need, Israel naturally sought an "ultimate deterrent" as early as the 1950s. Israeli governments under Prime Minister David Ben-Gurion and his successors considered a nuclear bomb to be a "weapon of last resort" intended to deter the state's foes from overrunning Israel in case the Israel Defense Forces (IDF) ever suffered a catastrophic defeat on the battlefield. With French industrial assistance, which was almost certainly extended in return for Israeli scientific assistance to France's own nuclear weapons program, Israel was able to put in place the infrastructure for a nuclear arms program no later than the early 1960s.

The Israeli program, of course, soon caught the eye of the United States. In light of America's strong nonproliferation agenda, the administrations of both Presidents John F. Kennedy and Lyndon Johnson attempted to entice Israel into signing the Nuclear Nonproliferation Treaty (NPT) in exchange for the supply of conventional arms, including antiaircraft missiles, tanks, and fighter-bombers.[3] Israel desperately wanted American arms, but stubbornly refused to give up its nuclear option by signing the NPT. Eventually, the United States and Israel, as part of their informal "security-for-autonomy" bargain (under whose terms the United States provided Israel with security benefits in the form of arms, while Israel provided the United States with autonomy benefits in the form of foreign policy concessions), worked out a mutually acceptable compromise.

The United States would provide Israel with the arms it required for its defense without asking the country to concede its nuclear option. Israel, in return, would give the United States a degree of control over its nuclear arsenal by consenting to keep its "bomb in the basement"—that is, Israel would not openly flaunt its nuclear option, so as not to undermine either American–Arab relations or America's global nonproliferation agenda. This deal was apparently sealed once and for all during a 1969 face-to-face meeting between President Richard Nixon and Prime Minister Golda Meir.[4]

Israeli Nuclear Arms and Deterrence in the Yom Kippur War

The first line of thought maintains that Israeli nuclear arms acted as a potent deterrent during the war.[5] Merely be possessing nuclear weapons, according to this line of thought, Israel inhibited Arab ambitions in the war. The essential claim is that, because Syria and Egypt feared the possibility of Israeli nuclear retribution, they did not threaten Israel proper, limiting the focus of their war aims to the Golan and Sinai, respectively. The following quote encapsulates this line of thought:

> [T]he walls of Jericho did not fall in 1973. They were not even close to falling, because the Arabs were rather careful. They planned a limited war on the margins of the occupied territory [i.e., the Golan and the Sinai], specifically not aimed at Israel's heartland and pre-1967 boundaries, in order to accomplish limited ends through . . . attrition and superpower intervention in their favor.[6]

This nuclear-induced caution, in other words, explains why, at the outset of the war, the Syrian army did not attempt to advance beyond the Golan, as well as why the Egyptian army did not attempt to strike more deeply into the Sinai, when the IDF did not possess sufficient forces along the front lines to rebuff them.

The problem with this line of thought is that no authoritative evidence, testimonial or documentary, has emerged to support it in the decades since the Yom Kippur War. The claim that the Arabs curbed their war aims out of fear of Israel's nuclear arsenal rests entirely upon inference, bolstered by the opinions of some American, Israeli, and Arab observers, none of whom has ever been in a position to know what was in the minds of Syrian and Egyptian decision makers in October 1973. This line of thought, in short, makes deductions about Arab intentions on the basis of Arab actions.

Judging intentions on the basis of actions, however, is a risky business. One can easily come up with a more plausible explanation for Syrian and Egyptian caution early in the war than the existence of Israeli nuclear arms. The Syrian army's lack of zeal in exploiting its initial gains on the southern Golan to advance into Israel proper almost certainly had more to do with a rigid command structure that looked askance at initiative from below than with any concern about Israeli nuclear retribution. In the absence of clear orders from above to continue the advance into Israel itself—a contingency that the Syrian army is unlikely to have given any real consideration in its prewar operational plan—its momentum simply petered out on the southern Golan as a result of heavy losses. Furthermore, in light of the stout resistance put up by the relatively small IDF forces on the southern Golan, even had the Syrian army given some thought to an offensive into Israel before the war, the Syrian regime may have concluded that to invade would have left the army strung out over long lines of communication and vulnerable to a devastating IDF counterattack, particularly from the air.

In the case of Egypt, it took the Egyptian army years of meticulous planning and preparation just to get across the Suez Canal and to establish shallow bridgeheads in the Sinai. A more ambitious prewar operational plan that included a deep strike into the Sinai from day one, let alone an offensive into Israel proper, was clearly beyond the capability of the Egyptian army. Indeed, later in the war, when the Egyptian army attempted to advance toward the Sinai's mountain passes, the IDF routed it in one of history's largest tank battles. And this defeat, in turn, left the Egyptian army vulnerable to an IDF counteroffensive over the canal, a counteroffensive that led to an Egyptian defeat in the war.

The bottom line here is that battlefield constraints, not Israeli nuclear weapons, offer the most plausible explanation for any limits placed on Arab war aims. In the absence of any authoritative testimonial or documentary evidence to the contrary, therefore, the assertion that Israeli nuclear arms curbed Syrian and Egyptian appetites in the war is no more than wishful thinking, a conclusion strengthened by the fact that adherents of this line of thought believe that nuclear proliferation in the Middle East would have a stabilizing effect on the region and/or that Israel should declare itself a nuclear power in order to buttress its deterrent posture.[7]

Israeli Nuclear Arms and Compellence in the Yom Kippur War

The second line of thought asserts that, during the early days of the Yom Kippur War, Israel compelled the United States to establish an arms pipeline to the IDF by actually brandishing its nuclear arms.[8] The Meir government, according to this version of events, discreetly placed its nuclear forces on alert sometime between October 7 and October 9—accounts differ on the precise timing of the alert—in order to signal to the Nixon administration that Israel had both the will and the wherewithal to use its nuclear stockpile to prevent an impending defeat at the hands of Syria and Egypt if the United States refused to set up an arms pipeline, one that would allow the IDF to reverse the tide of the war. The Meir government, in the language of one of the most notorious proponents of this account of events, literally "blackmailed" the Nixon administration into supporting Israel in the Yom Kippur War.[9]

This line of thought—like the first—is not backed up by any authoritative evidence, testimonial or documentary, unless one considers hearsay and idle speculation to qualify as such.[10] Leaving aside the fact that no verifiable evidence that Israel actually put its nuclear forces on alert during the war has thus far come to light, the "facts" as laid out by those observers who claim otherwise are inconsistent with the established facts. First, reliable recollections of the meeting at which the decision to place Israel's nuclear forces on alert was supposedly taken indicate that the only decision maker in favor of such a move was Defense Minister Moshe Dayan. All others present, including Meir herself, unanimously and categorically rejected this alternative.[11] Second, by October 13, the date on which the Nixon administration initiated an arms air- and sealift to Israel, the Meir government had accepted an American proposal for a cease-fire, while the Arabs and their Soviet patron had not done so. Indeed, on at least two occasions during the war, Secretary of State Henry Kissinger made it perfectly clear to his own staff that the principal reason that the United States decided to send arms to Israel was that the Arabs, with the support of the Soviet Union, which had already begun a large-scale air- and sealift to its clients, dismissed this call for a cease-fire.[12] The United States, to put it differently, simply refused to abandon its client in a time of need.

American Nuclear Arms and the Yom Kippur War

The one and only undisputed instance in which nuclear arms played any sort of role in the Yom Kippur War occurred at the tail end of hostilities—and it involved American, not Israeli, nuclear weapons. Ostensibly in response to Soviet threats and preparations to intervene in the war on behalf of Egypt, which allegedly involved the movement of nuclear arms to the region, after the IDF had surrounded the Egyptian Third Army, one of the two Egyptian army corps participating in the fighting, the United States placed its own armed forces, including Strategic Air Command (SAC), which controls the country's nuclear-armed intercontinental ballistic missiles and its nuclear-armed bombers, on a heightened state of alert, moving from Defense Condition (DEFCON) 5, the normal peacetime state of readiness, to DEFCON 3, a heightened state of readiness. The alert lasted from October 25 until October 26, at least insofar as concerned SAC.

A senior Soviet diplomat later revealed that the Soviet Union never intended to intervene in the war.[13] The Nixon administration was apparently aware of this fact at the time. Kissinger remarked that:

> The crazy bastard [Nixon] really made a mess with the Russians. . . . [Did not] you listen to his [October 26] press statement? . . . [W]e had information of massive movement of Soviet forces. That is a lie.[14]

CHAPTER 3

For this reason, some Israeli observers contend that the Nixon administration's real purpose in putting its forces on DEFCON 3 was to place additional pressure on Israel to release its grip on the Third Army in order to curry favor with Egypt and to reduce Soviet influence in the Middle East.[15] Whatever the truth here, the Nixon administration's move to declare DEFCON 3 almost certainly had no impact on Israeli decision making, as the Meir government had already calculated that it had no choice but to accommodate the Nixon administration as part of the security-for-autonomy bargain.

Summary

The evidence that has surfaced to date does not support the conclusion that Israeli nuclear arms had any tangible impact on the Yom Kippur War. The limited ambitions of Syria and Egypt in the war were almost certainly due to their evaluations of their conventional military capabilities versus those of the IDF, not to fear of Israeli nuclear arms. For its part, the United States did not set up an arms pipeline to Israel as a result of Israeli nuclear blackmail. It initiated an air- and sealift to Israel only after the latter had agreed to a cease-fire arrangement after a week of hostilities, an arrangement that the Arabs and Soviets rejected in order to continue to prosecute the war.

The assertion that Israeli nuclear arms deterred Syria and Egypt during the Yom Kippur War seems to be a case in which a political agenda—in this case, an agenda in favor of nuclear weapons proliferation in the Middle East—has influenced the analysis of historical events. Likewise, the assertion that Israel employed its nuclear arms to blackmail the United States into setting up an arms pipeline during the war also appears to be an example of ideological bias winning out over detached evaluation. Is it just a coincidence that those observers who trumpet this perspective are, to put it politely, no friends of Israel? Extraordinary claims, it is often said, require extraordinary evidence. Not only have the proponents of both lines of thought failed to provide such extraordinary evidence, but they have also failed to provide any convincing evidence whatsoever.

Part II
Battle

Retreat heralds defeat.
Talmud, Sota

4

Israeli Combined Arms Warfare

The Israel Defense Forces (IDF) emerged from the 1973 Yom Kippur War as the undisputed victor over the armies of its Arab foes. Despite suffering serious reverses on both the Golan and Sinai fronts during the opening days of the war, the IDF not only recovered quickly to inflict on Arab armies losses in men and machines that far exceeded its own, but it also captured considerably more territory than it had relinquished during the fighting. In the north, the IDF first swept the Syrian army entirely from the Israeli-controlled portion of the Golan and then proceeded to conquer a swath of territory inside Syria. In the south, though the Egyptian army remained ensconced in a strip of territory in the Sinai throughout the war, the IDF eventually crossed the Suez Canal and seized a sizable chunk of land inside Egypt proper. By the war's end, the IDF had advanced to within striking range of Damascus and Cairo, the Syrian and Egyptian capitals, respectively.

Nevertheless, the IDF has come under intense and widespread criticism for its performance during the Yom Kippur War. Perhaps the most frequent criticism leveled against the IDF asserts that it shunned the practice of traditional combined arms warfare in favor of a nontraditional force structure and war-fighting doctrine that relied overwhelmingly on tanks and aircraft at the expense of infantry, artillery, engineers, and logistics. The following are three rather typical examples of this particular criticism:

> [The IDF's] attempts to use tanks and air power [sic] without strong support from the infantry or artillery branches ... led to many of its problems during the 1973 war and showed [it] the need for a more balanced combined arms approach.[1]

> Both the [Sinai Campaign] and the Six-Day War had left the [IDF] with the impression that wars on the ground were won by armor

CHAPTER 4

> [i.e., tanks] and armor alone. As a result, [it] failed to develop an integrated infantry–armor doctrine, and effectively eschewed the use of infantry. . . . Part of the IDF's problem was its overreliance on armor; another equally important component was its underreliance on artillery. The latter was related to the fact that . . . the [Israel Air Force] had gained air superiority within the first few days of [previous] conflict[s].[2]
>
> The IDF of 1973 was not built organizationally or mentally for an absolute commitment to joint operations. The realization of the paramount value of combined-arms [sic] combat was one of the IDF's bitterest lessons of the Yom Kippur War. . .[3]

Many more examples could be added to the list, of course, but these three—the first two by American military analysts, the third by an Israeli tank battalion commander on the Sinai front—suffice to reveal the essence of the criticism with respect to the IDF's force structure and war-fighting doctrine during the war.

This criticism, the truth be known, certainly has much merit behind it. As a consequence of its previous experience, particularly during the 1967 Six-Day War, the IDF built up its tank and aircraft orders of battle at the expense of its infantry, artillery, engineer, and logistics orders of battle in the years prior to the Yom Kippur War. Furthermore, the IDF's war-fighting doctrine before the war at both the tactical (micro) and operational (macro) levels of warfare assigned decisive roles to tanks and aircraft, foregoing a more symmetrical approach to the integration of combat arms.[4]

Be that as it may, this criticism is based primarily on the IDF's performance during the first few days of the Yom Kippur War, especially on the Sinai front, when it scrambled to block the Syrian and Egyptian assaults with the meager forces that were deployed in the north and south at the commencement of hostilities. Indeed, many of the IDF's critics concede that its shortcomings in combined arms warfare were the result not only of its faulty force structure and war-fighting doctrine before the war, but also of the circumstances that it faced at the outbreak of hostilities. Once the IDF recovered from its initial shock and stabilized the fronts, its performance in respect of combined arms warfare displayed marked improvement on both the tactical and operational levels.

A balanced, sober assessment of the IDF's practice of combined arms warfare in the Yom Kippur War first requires that this concept be defined and illustrated in general terms for the sake of clarity. Next, it is necessary to describe and analyze the IDF's practice of combined arms warfare on both the Golan and Sinai fronts. Cooperation (or lack thereof) between the Israel Air Force (IAF) and IDF ground forces at both the tactical and operational levels became a very contentious issue at home and abroad after the war, so this dimension of Israel's combined arms warfare experience demands separate consideration. Once these tasks are complete, it becomes possible to ascertain the impact combined arms warfare had on the IDF's fortunes during the war.

The Concept of Combined Arms Warfare

The United States Army, which has probably done more thinking about the nature of warfare than any other military organization, past or present, defines combined arms warfare succinctly as:

> [T]he synchronized and simultaneous application of arms [e.g., tank, infantry, artillery] to achieve an effect greater than if each arm was used separately or sequentially.[5]

Combined arms warfare is intended to enhance an army's performance on the battlefield, regardless of whether that army is engaged in an offensive or a defensive campaign and regardless of whether it is engaged in a maneuver or an attrition campaign.[6]

Combined arms warfare has two distinct components: force structure and war-fighting doctrine. Force structure refers to the types of units and weapons fielded by an army. The following are a few examples of the force structure component at different levels of unit aggregation: an infantry company equipped with rifle, machine gun, mortar, and antitank missile platoons; a tank battalion with an attached mechanized infantry company; a tank brigade composed of tank and mechanized infantry battalions; a tank division consisting of tank and mechanized infantry brigades and artillery and engineering battalions; and a corps or an army made up of tank and infantry divisions, artillery brigades, engineering battalions, as well as air and naval units. The force structure component, in other words, is relevant at both the tactical and operational levels of warfare.

War-fighting doctrine refers to the way in which an army employs its force structure on the battlefield. The following are a few examples of the war-fighting doctrine component applied to hypothetical battle scenarios at different levels of unit aggregation: an artillery battery lays down suppressive fire as tank and infantry platoons assault an enemy strongpoint; a mechanized infantry company engages enemy antitank missile teams while a tank battalion engages enemy tanks; an infantry brigade screens an engineering battalion from enemy infantry as engineers construct a bridge over a water obstacle; a tank brigade pins down enemy infantry while an infantry division advances toward the enemy infantry; artillery battalions lay down suppressive fire as engineer battalions open gaps through an enemy defensive line for tank and infantry divisions to exploit; and a corps or an army receives air support as it defends its frontline positions. Like the force structure component of combined arms warfare, the war-fighting doctrine component is relevant at both the tactical and operational levels of warfare.

The keys to combined arms warfare at both the tactical and operational levels of warfare, in short, are symmetry and integration. The practice of traditional combined arms warfare requires not only a balanced mix of different kinds of units and weapons, but also a war-fighting doctrine that coordinates their employment to mutual advantage. If prepared for and implemented properly, the traditional approach to combined arms warfare is an effective force multiplier on the battlefield.

Combined Arms Warfare in the IDF Before the Yom Kippur War

In the Six-Day War, the IDF not only crushed the Egyptian, Jordanian, and Syrian armies in just a few days, but it also captured the Sinai in the south, Judea and Samaria in the east, and the Golan in the north. Israelis in general, and the Israeli defense establishment in particular, concluded that this tremendous victory should be attributed almost exclusively to the actions of the IAF and the IDF tank corps. The IAF destroyed virtually the entire Egyptian, Jordanian, and Syrian air forces at their bases during the first hours of hostilities, thus assuring itself of air superiority throughout the war. IDF tank brigades swept all of the Arab armies before them. Infantry, artillery, engineers, and logistics, according to the Israeli assessment, had only minor supporting roles in the triumph.

This view had consequences for the IDF's force structure and war-fighting doctrine. Already favored in the IDF's procurement plans well before 1967, tanks and aircraft received even more emphasis after the war. The IDF's tank inventory increased by roughly 100 percent and its fighter-bomber inventory by more than 50 percent between 1967 and 1973, not to mention that their quality improved dramatically as well with the acquisition of the most modern American weapons. Indeed, the IAF's acquisition of state-of-the-art American fighter-bombers, which replaced most of its antiquated French aircraft, increased its striking power several times over.[7] Outlays on the IAF alone ate up over 50 percent of the Israeli defense budget in the years prior to the Yom Kippur War.[8]

Other IDF branches had to make do with what was left of the budget after tank corps and air force needs were addressed by the defense establishment. The capabilities of these branches, therefore, either remained stagnant or withered over time. The mechanized infantry went to war in 1973 with only a limited number of modern armored personnel carriers (APCs), and most of both the mechanized and nonmechanized infantry entered hostilities with antiquated rifles and antitank weapons. Furthermore, the quality of the mechanized infantry's manpower had deteriorated during the interwar period.[9] The artillery branch had roughly the same number of tubes in 1973 as it had in 1967, even if their overall quality had improved somewhat with the acquisition of small numbers of modern American self-propelled guns.[10] The engineering branch did not possess enough vehicles to move its equipment around the battlefield, nor did the logistics branch possess enough tank transporters to move quickly the required number of tanks to the battlefield. And many of those tanks were not ready for battle on the eve of hostilities, because the IDF's logistics branch lacked sufficient resources.[11]

The IDF's war-fighting doctrine evolved along a parallel track during the years from 1967 to 1973. The Israeli defense establishment concluded that tanks—whether the IDF was on the offensive or the defensive, whether it was engaged in a maneuver or an attrition campaign—did not need much in the way of infantry or artillery support. Mechanized and nonmechanized infantry would be employed mainly to mop up and secure the battlefield after the tanks had won the day. Suppressive fire from artillery would not be necessary on a large scale, because the defense establishment was convinced that the IAF's fighter-bombers would act as "flying artillery" in support of the tanks as soon as air superiority had been won—and the defense establishment took it for granted that the IAF would quickly achieve air superiority in the next war. The roles of the engineering and logistics branches in the IDF's war-fighting doctrine received no in-depth consideration from the defense establishment from 1967 to 1973.

This nontraditional vision of combined arms warfare was itself based on a number of assumptions, collectively termed "the concept," held by the defense establishment about the circumstances under which the next war would break out.¹² A first assumption held that the Arabs would not initiate a war that they could not win. A second assumption held that the Arabs would not begin a war until they could neutralize Israeli airpower by striking at IAF bases in Israel proper. And a third assumption held that Israeli military intelligence, A'MAN, would in any case provide at least 48 hours of advanced warning of an any attack.

All three of these assumptions turned out to be erroneous. The Arabs were willing to suffer a battlefield defeat in order to achieve a diplomatic victory; they were willing to sacrifice their armies in order to spark a diplomatic process that they believed would lead to the return of the Golan and Sinai. The Arabs had also devised a sophisticated operational plan to neutralize Israeli airpower that did not involve strikes against IAF bases. Instead, they would construct highly sophisticated integrated air defense systems (IADS) composed of large numbers of surface-to-air missile (SAM) and antiaircraft artillery (AAA) batteries on both fronts to blunt the effects of Israeli airpower. And, lastly, A'MAN would not in the event provide a clear war warning 48 hours in advance of the Arab attack. Though it monitored the deployment of the Egyptian and Syrian armies along the cease-fire lines for weeks before the attack, and though it informed both IDF general headquarters (GHQ) and the Israeli government that the Arabs had the ability to launch an attack given their present deployments along the fronts several days in advance of the attack, it continued to insist that the probability of an Arab attack in the fall of 1973 was quite low.

For their part, both IDF GHQ and the Israeli government, like A'MAN, chose to focus on Arab intentions rather than capabilities. Hence, they did not authorize a full-scale mobilization and deployment of the IDF's reserve formations, which constituted the bulk of Israel's fighting power, until literally a few hours before the commencement of hostilities. Not until an unimpeachable intelligence source had unequivocally confirmed that Egypt and Syria intended to launch an attack very shortly did Israel take this step.

Consequently, at approximately 2:00 PM on October 6, when the Syrian and Egyptian armies opened fire simultaneously on the Golan and in the Sinai, respectively, the IDF faced grossly lopsided force ratios on both fronts.¹³ On the Golan, the Syrians had a roughly 5:1 advantage in tanks (an 8:1 advantage counting their second-echelon tanks), a 10:1 advantage in infantry, and a 12–13:1 advantage in artillery tubes along the forward line of contact.¹⁴ In the Sinai, the Egyptians had a roughly 14:1 advantage in tanks, an 80:1 advantage in infantry, and a

40:1 advantage in artillery tubes along the forward line of contact.[15] The IDF's skewed force structure and war-fighting doctrine, combined with its lack of readiness for the coming war, would result in disastrous consequences for it during the opening days of the war.

Combined Arms Warfare on the Golan Front

The IDF's war on the northern front can be divided into three distinctive phases: a defensive phase from October 6 through October 10 to clear the Golan of Syrian forces, an offensive phase from October 11 through October 14 to acquire additional territory in Syria proper, and a second defensive phase from October 15 through October 24, when a stable cease-fire came into effect, to hold onto this newly captured territory. At the outset of hostilities, the IDF had the better part of two high-quality tank brigades (the southern of the two was less one tank battalion), a series of small hilltop strongpoints manned by high-quality infantry, a handful of artillery batteries, and some mechanized infantry and engineering forces to meet the Syrian onslaught of three infantry divisions, three tank brigades, more than 100 artillery batteries, and assorted engineering forces (with two additional tank divisions close by in the rear).[16]

The Syrian army launched a two-pronged offensive across the 1967 cease-fire line. Its main thrust was aimed at the southern part of the Golan, with a more limited (but still very potent) thrust aimed at the northern part of the plateau.[17] IDF ground forces on the Golan were better prepared to wage a defensive struggle against an invader than their counterparts in the Sinai. The high-quality infantrymen on the front line not only defended themselves and harassed Syrian columns that bypassed them, but they also served as forward observers for artillery barrages and air strikes against rear-echelon targets.[18] Some of the strongpoints held out until relieved later in the fighting, while those in danger of being overwhelmed by the Syrian army were evacuated in an orderly manner. Only one would fall to the Syrian army.

On the northern Golan, the Syrian offensive got nowhere. A spectacular mobile defense waged by the IDF tank brigade stationed in the area stopped much larger Syrian ground forces in their tracks for several days, destroying hundreds of tanks and APCs in the process. On the southern Golan, to the contrary, the Syrians were able to break through the IDF tank brigade in this sector. Though this brigade took a very heavy toll of attacking Syrian tanks and APCs, the gross imbalance in numbers between attacker and defender proved decisive here.

CHAPTER 4

A breakthrough into Israel proper—which had now become a very real possibility, even if was not part of Syria's prewar operational plan—was only prevented by the delaying actions of the remnants of this brigade, IAF air strikes against rear-echelon supply convoys, and the timely intervention of the first reserve forces, which arrived within 12 hours of the outbreak of hostilities, as well as Syrian hesitance.[19]

By October 8, the IDF had amassed enough forces on the Golan—significant elements of three tank divisions—to begin a counterattack against the Syrian army in order to push it back beyond the "Purple Line," the title given to the 1967 cease-fire line. This multidivisional effort on the southern Golan steadily drove the Syrian army out of Israeli-controlled territory. Indeed, by October 10, the Syrian army held only one position inside the Israeli portion of the Golan, a strongpoint on Mount Hermon, which the IDF would recapture late in the war.

Though tanks spearheaded the defensive effort from October 6 through October 10, the IDF did practice traditional combined arms warfare to a certain extent during the opening days of the war on the Golan front. At the tactical level, the hilltop strongpoints acted as forward observation posts in directing artillery barrages and air strikes against targets in the Syrian army's rear. Artillery engaged in suppressive fire in support of IDF tank forces whenever possible, while engineering forces created or demolished obstacles to slow the Syrian advance.[20] At the operational level, the tanks, mechanized and nonmechanized infantry, artillery, and engineers of three divisions engaged in a coordinated effort to drive the Syrian army from Israeli-controlled territory. And air support, though acting only in loose coordination with the ground forces, proved important in halting the Syrian advance on the southern Golan.[21]

On October 11, the IDF began a counteroffensive into Syria.[22] The principal purpose of this attack was to capture a swath of territory inside Syria to act as a bargaining chip in postwar negotiations, particularly in light of the fact that Egypt had managed to conquer a chunk of territory in the Sinai. Traditional combined arms warfare played a prominent role in this counteroffensive, as the IDF "advanced in a manner designed to minimize casualties by using heavy tank and artillery fire to open the way rather than making costly armor charges."[23] Mechanized and parachute infantry, engineering forces, and IAF fighter-bombers also performed prominent tasks in the IDF's attack. On October 14, the IDF halted its counteroffensive, when its long-range artillery had moved to within range of the outskirts of Damascus.

From October 15 through October 24, the Syrian army, along with Iraqi and Jordanian expeditionary forces, engaged in local counterattacks against the Israeli enclave. The IDF repulsed all of these attacks through the practice of traditional combined arms warfare. Tank, mechanized and parachute infantry, artillery, and engineering forces worked in unison to beat back assaults by Arab tank and infantry forces. The only Israeli-initiated attack during the last 10 days of fighting on the Golan front involved the recapture of the IDF intelligence-gathering facility on Mount Hermon.[24] Infantry forces advancing from above and below, with artillery and air support, won a bloody triumph over Syrian special forces ensconced there in a feat of traditional combined arms warfare.

Combined Arms Warfare on the Sinai Front

The IDF's war on the southern front can also be divided into distinct phases: a largely defensive phase from October 6 through October 14 to halt the Egyptian penetration in the Sinai and an offensive phase from October 15 through October 24 to cross the Suez Canal in order to seize territory in Egypt proper. When the Egyptian army initiated its assault on Sinai, the IDF had only a few hundred, low-quality infantrymen, a few dozen tanks, and a handful of artillery tubes immediately adjacent to the waterline to oppose the five infantry divisions of the first wave, which included hundreds of tanks and APCs and which were supported by about 2,000 artillery tubes.[25]

The IDF's infantrymen were holed up in a series of widely scattered strongpoints alongside the Suez Canal, known rather grandiosely as the Bar Lev Line (after the former chief of staff who had authorized their construction). On the one hand, the Bar Lev Line was not built to withstand a large-scale, cross-canal attack. But, on the other hand, the Israeli government demanded that the IDF prevent an Egyptian "land grab" on the Israeli side of the Suez Canal that could result in a diplomatic setback for Israel. Thus, the Israeli defense establishment, rather than permit the infantrymen in the strongpoints to withdraw to safety in case of a large-scale assault, decided that they must remain in place in order to harass the invading Egyptians and to act as forward observers for artillery fire and air support until they could be relieved by an IDF counterattack.

This forward defense concept, combined with the Israeli ethos of never abandoning men in the field, created a harrowing scenario for the IDF at the outset of the war. The low quality of the infantrymen on the Bar Lev Line, as well as the immense volume of firepower thrown at them by the Egyptian army, meant that the strongpoints could neither effectively harass the infantry divisions crossing the canal nor effectively call in artillery barrages or air strikes (even had artillery or air support been a realistic option). Moreover, with many of them surrounded and under siege, the strongpoints began to call for assistance.

The IDF responded with small-scale "tank charges" toward the canal in an effort to relieve the strongpoints. These tank charges were not supported by artillery fire, as the few guns near the front were under heavy counterbattery fire themselves, or by infantry, as most of the infantry in Sinai had been drained off either to protect rear-area installations or to counter Egyptian special forces troops transported into the Israeli rear via helicopters, or by fighter-bombers, as the IAF's squadrons were busy with other tasks. Attacking into the teeth of extremely heavy and coordinated artillery, tank, and antitank missile and rocket fire without any supporting arms, the three tank brigades committed to battle on that first day lost approximately 150 tanks (closer to 175 if mechanical breakdowns and accidents are counted as well), with precious little to show for their efforts.[26] Though tanks did manage to link up with a few of the strongpoints and to evacuate some of the wounded, all of the Bar Lev Line positions, except for one in the extreme north, along the Mediterranean coast, eventually fell to the Egyptian army, with most of the infantrymen in them either killed or captured.

While the IDF's regular tank division was fighting to relieve the strongpoints and to contain the Egyptian bridgeheads along the canal, two reserve tank divisions arrived in Sinai in less than two days, despite a lack of tank transporters and other logistical problems. The mobilization and deployment of tanks took priority over infantry and artillery. Once IDF GHQ believed that a sufficient number of tanks had been accumulated along the front, it authorized a multidivisional counterattack on October 8. The IDF, after all, had been built primarily for offensive maneuver warfare, and its war-fighting doctrine emphasized a counterattack at the earliest possible moment.

This counterattack, averred GHQ, would roll up the Egyptian bridgeheads from north to south and, perhaps, capture a bridge, which the IDF could then use to cross the canal into Egypt proper.[27] This optimistic assessment proved to be divorced from reality. The counterattack quickly turned into a debacle. Though the IDF probably gave as good as it got from the Egyptian army, two of its tank battalions were more or less completely destroyed during the fighting, in part by infantry equipped with antitank missiles and rockets. When the IDF finally halted its counterattack, the Egyptians had not been dislodged from any of their positions in the Sinai.

The counterattack violated the most basic principles of traditional combined arms warfare at both the tactical and operational levels: symmetry and integration. Infantry, artillery, and air support were sparse at best. The lead division in the attack, for example, had been stripped of its mechanized infantry and had only a handful of artillery tubes to engage in suppressive fire.[28] Despite the battering that the IDF's tanks had absorbed on October 6–7, they once again charged into the teeth of Egyptian defenses on their own, with predictable results.

On the Golan front, the lack of infantry and artillery forces did not constitute a major problem, because the challenge faced by the IDF came mainly from Syrian tanks. The hilly, rocky terrain made it difficult for the Syrian army to deploy antitank missiles and rockets, so these weapons played almost no role here. In the Sinai, with its largely flat terrain, to the contrary, antitank missiles and rockets had a very prominent role in Egypt's operational plan. The paucity of infantry and artillery during the opening days of the war, therefore, had grave consequences for the IDF's fortunes here, as infantry and artillery were the most effective means for countering these weapons.

While not a failure of combined arms warfare per se, command and control (C^2) problems throughout the October 8 counterattack added to the IDF's woes. The two tank divisions involved in the fighting did not coordinate their operations at any point in the battle, and one of them essentially went around in circles for much of the battle as a result of confused and contradictory orders issued by IDF GHQ and IDF southern command headquarters (HQ).[29]

Bruised by its setback in the counterattack, the IDF went back on the defensive from October 9 through October 14. During this period, its force structure and war-fighting doctrine accommodated themselves to the lessons of the first three days of battle: sufficient numbers of infantrymen and artillery tubes were incorporated into the tank divisions. Damaged tanks were repaired and returned to service. And, from this point forward, the IDF would no longer engage in unsupported tank charges. Rather, tanks would advance cautiously, and in tandem with suppressive fire from infantry and artillery, mindful of the advantages of traditional combined arms warfare.[30]

From October 9 through October 13, both the IDF and the Egyptian army were largely content to hold and consolidate their positions, satisfying themselves with limited probes along the front line.

CHAPTER 4

The skirmishes that erupted as a consequence of these probes invariably ended in the IDF's favor, because of its clear superiority in maneuver warfare.[31] During this period, IDF GHQ decided to wait for the Egyptian army to launch a large-scale offensive in an attempt to break out of its canal-side bridgeheads, which GHQ expected to come shortly, before initiating a cross-canal offensive of the IDF's own.

The opportunity to engage in a major mobile tank battle occurred on October 14. Partly in order to reach the key Sinai mountain passes and partly in order to reduce the pressure on its faltering Syrian ally in the north, the Egyptian army launched a multidivisional offensive along a number of different axes. To make a long story short, the Egyptian army suffered a crushing defeat that day, losing 200–250 tanks. IDF tank losses stood at 10–20.[32] At the tactical level, suppressive fire from IDF infantry and artillery countered the Egyptian infantry's antitank missiles and rockets, turning them into a nonentity during the battle, while Israeli tanks dealt harsh blows to their Egyptian counterparts. At the operational level, IAF fighter-bombers cooperated with IDF tanks, infantry, and artillery to halt and scatter any Egyptian forces that moved beyond the range of the Egyptian army's IADS. In the October 14 tank battle, the largest in history, except for the Battle of Kursk during the Second World War, the IDF performed a genuine feat of traditional combined arms warfare.

If the October 14 tank battle constituted the first turning point of the war on the southern front, the IDF's cross-canal counterattack, begun on October 15, constituted the second turning point. From this date until the end of the war, the IDF would be on the offensive, the Egyptian army on the defensive. The crossing operation itself was another feat of traditional combined arms warfare at both the tactical and operational levels. Tanks, mechanized and nonmechanized infantry, artillery, and engineers all worked hand in hand, first, to break through to the waterline and, second, to ferry tank and infantry forces across the canal.[33] Essentially, IDF tank brigades, infantry battalions, and artillery battalions fought a bloody but ultimately victorious battle, particularly at a place called the Chinese Farm (which had actually been a Japanese agricultural station prior to the Six-Day War), to break through to the waterline. This success initially allowed engineers to ferry parachute infantry and a number of tanks across the canal on boats and pontoons, creating a small bridgehead on the Egyptian side of the canal. After several days of additional hard fighting, the IDF expanded and solidified its bridgehead on both sides of the canal, eventually transferring the better part of three tank divisions into Egypt proper over bridges that its engineers had constructed across the canal.

Once across the Suez Canal, mixed tank and infantry columns immediately began to fan out, especially to smash SAM and AAA batteries.[34] IDF artillery fire from the Israeli side of the canal also hit batteries located close to the waterline. These efforts resulted in the destruction of large sections of the Egyptian army's IADS, opening up undefended flight corridors, which in turn allowed IAF fighter-bombers to provide air support to advancing IDF columns. By the time a more or less stable cease-fire came into effect on the southern front, the IDF had advanced to within about 100 kilometers of Cairo, had surrounded the Egyptian Third Army (one of the two corps involved in the Egyptian offensive), and had captured more territory on the Egyptian side of the canal than Egypt held on the Israeli side. The practice of traditional combined arms warfare at both the tactical and operational levels had once again proven itself.

Combined Arms Warfare: Air–Ground Cooperation

In the months prior to the Yom Kippur War, the IAF concluded that it would need 48 hours to take command of the air at the outset of hostilities if given a clear war warning 36–48 hours ahead of time.[35] The air force preferred to launch a preemptive strike to achieve this objective, but it asserted that it could still accomplish the objective if the Arabs attacked first. The IAF's main priorities at the start of hostilities would be to ensure air supremacy over Israel itself, so that the IDF's reserve formations could mobilize and deploy for battle unmolested by Arab airpower, and to achieve air superiority over the battlefield(s), so that it could then provide air support as needed to IDF ground forces. To accomplish these two tasks, the IAF developed intricate operational plans to demolish the Syrian and Egyptian IADSs—operational plans that included cooperation with IDF long-range artillery—as well as to pin down the Syrian and Egyptian air forces through a combination of air-to-air combat and air base attacks.

The IAF's prewar thinking assigned a rather low priority to support of the ground forces. Indeed, its intent to take command of the air at the outset of hostilities meant that the ground forces would be largely, if not entirely, devoid of air support during the first two days of war. The IDF's ground forces, reasoned both the IAF and IDF GHQ, would be able to hold their positions against the Arab armies until the air force could join the battle in a decisive way. The IAF had developed an operational plan to deal with a worst-case scenario in which IDF ground forces required immediate, large-scale air support to hold their positions, but it sat in a file cabinet somewhere gathering dust; the air force never gave it much consideration.

Despite the fact that Israel had only a few hours of warning that war was about to erupt in the north and south, the IAF still possessed the capability to launch a preemptive strike, albeit one more modest in scope than the one envisaged in its elaborate prewar operational plans. Be that as it may, the Israeli government vetoed a preemptive strike for two major reasons. First, and foremost, it feared the loss of American military and diplomatic support if the IDF opened fire before the Arab armies.[36] And, second, IDF GHQ had assured the government that Israel would win the war even if the Syrian and Egyptian armies struck the initial blow.

Opinions are mixed as to the impact an IAF preemptive strike might have had on the IDF's fortunes in the war. On the one hand, some military analysts believe that even a limited strike would have completely changed the complexion of the war by shifting the operational initiative to the IDF. Two analysts, for example, calculated that, had Israel seized the initiative, the IAF could have knocked out 90 percent of the Syrian and Egyptian SAM batteries "in a period of three to six hours for the loss of under [10] aircraft." With air superiority over the Golan and Sinai thus virtually assured as a consequence, according to this line of reasoning, IAF intervention in the ground battle would have been swift and massive, its fighter-bombers dropping "[3,000] tons of bombs on enemy targets before the Arab attack reached full strength."[37] Other analysts, in contrast, believe that a preemptive strike, regardless of its scope, would not have made an appreciable difference in how the war unfolded in the first few days.[38] Which perspective has greater merit, of course, must remain in the realm of speculation.

Regardless of the fact that the war began under the worst-case scenario, the IAF devoted the lion's share of its resources during the opening days to its prewar priorities: securing Israeli airspace and overcoming Arab IADSs. On the morning of October 7, the IAF initiated a large-scale attack against the Egyptian IADS based on its prewar operational plan. The attack initially made headway, but it was soon canceled, because of the ominous situation on the Golan front.[39] The IAF then attempted to attack the Syrian IADS, again based on its prewar operational plan. This attack, which resulted in heavy aircraft losses as a result of outdated intelligence information and uncoordinated execution, failed to dent, let alone destroy, Syrian air defenses.[40] Hence, the Syrian IADS survived the war mainly intact and the Egyptian IADS was only overcome late in the fighting, largely as a result of the actions of IDF ground forces.

The inability to knock out the Syrian and Egyptian IADSs early on in the war seriously impeded the IAF's ability to engage in traditional combined arms warfare with the ground forces throughout much of the war.[41] On the Golan front, in order to avert a potential Syrian breakthrough into Israel proper, the IAF did act as flying artillery out of extremely dire necessity during the first few days of the war, engaging in a high-tempo campaign against the Syrian army. Its strikes against rear-echelon, soft-skinned supply convoys were helpful in slowing the momentum of the Syrian offensive, but at a very considerable cost in aircraft lost to air defenses. After the IDF advanced into Syria, the IAF's efforts on the Golan slackened considerably in order to conserve the air force's fighter-bomber fleet.

During the first days of war, IDF ground forces on the Sinai front received less effective air support than those on the Golan front. The support the IAF furnished here was aimed primarily at countering the infiltration of Egyptian special forces, at relieving the Bar Lev Line strongpoints, and at knocking out the Egyptian bridges. Cooperation between the IAF and IDF ground forces succeeded in eliminating the special forces threat, as the air force shot down many troop-carrying helicopters and ferried IDF "commando-hunter" squads to deal with those Egyptians who managed to land behind the front lines. In both of the latter cases, however, not only did air support prove very ineffective, but it also entailed significant losses to the Egyptian IADS, which is why these efforts were soon suspended. The IDF counterattack on October 8, as noted above, received little air support.[42] After the first few days of hostilities, the IAF limited its support to the ground forces almost exclusively to areas that fell outside of the Egyptian IADS, as in the October 14 tank battle. Only after IDF ground forces crossed the canal and began to overrun Egyptian SAM batteries did the IAF really enter the land war in a more significant manner, helping to seal the fate of the Egyptian Third Army.

Overall, the IAF and IDF ground forces did not act as an efficient combined arms warfare team at either the tactical or operational levels throughout much of the war, a few instances to the contrary notwithstanding. The inability to overcome the Syrian and Egyptian IADSs at the outset of hostilities certainly goes a long way toward explaining the deficiencies in cooperation between the IAF and IDF ground forces. But other reasons obtained as well. Because the IAF assigned a low priority to support of IDF ground forces before the Yom Kippur War, it did not develop much in the way of a C^2 infrastructure to ensure close cooperation with those forces.[43] And, for its part, IDF GHQ, convinced of the IAF's invincibility as a result of its performance in the Six-Day War, did not grasp the true limitations of airpower.

CHAPTER 4

Summary

Critics of the IDF's practice of combined arms warfare during the Yom Kippur War tend to focus on how the war began rather than on how it ended. Unquestionably, both the IDF's force structure and war-fighting doctrine before the war were heavily slanted in favor of tanks and aircraft and against infantry, artillery, engineers, and logistics. And, undoubtedly, this nontraditonal force structure and war-fighting doctrine contributed significantly to serious IDF losses in tanks and aircraft during the first days of war. Still, these tank and aircraft losses were incurred largely as a result of the IDF's general unpreparedness for war, which meant that it had to hurl its tanks and aircraft mainly unsupported at the Syrian and Egyptian armies in a desperate containment effort, because a few tank brigades and its fighter-bomber squadrons were the only forces it had immediately available to counter their offensives.

Whatever the case, to its credit, the IDF quickly improvised a force structure and war-fighting doctrine that allowed it to engage in traditional combined arms warfare at both the tactical and operational levels, at least insofar as concerned its ground forces. No less an authority than the officer in charge of the United State Army's Training and Doctrine (TRADOC) Command at the time of the Yom Kippur War remarked that:

> The Israelis demonstrated [that] it is possible to operate successfully in the face of highly lethal weapons by effective use of the combined arms team[:] that is[,] tanks supported by mechanized infantry, self-propelled artillery, and self-propelled air defense weapons.[44]

At the operational level, the IDF's counteroffensives into Syria and Egypt constituted impressive feats of traditional combined arms warfare.

Furthermore, even when traditional combined arms warfare was clearly absent in a direct sense, such as in the lack of close cooperation between the IAF and IDF ground forces throughout much of the war, it might still be argued that it existed to a certain extent in an indirect sense. The IAF, after all, kept Israel's skies clean, allowing the IDF's reserve formations to mobilize and deploy for battle swiftly. It also kept the Arab air forces pinned down throughout the war—through a combination of air-to-air combat and frequent air base attacks—so IDF ground forces were able to function essentially unimpeded by Arab air strikes. And, strategic attacks against targets in the Arab hinterland (e.g., fuel depots and port facilities)—in which the Israel Navy (IN) also had a hand—served to divert at least some Arab forces away from the front, especially on the Golan.

Finally, it must be noted that traditional combined arms warfare did not constitute a panacea for the IDF. This practice, to be sure, cut down on the IDF's losses in men and machines, but it certainly did not eliminate them. Even after it adopted a force structure and war-fighting doctrine compatible with traditional combined arms warfare, the IDF nevertheless still suffered substantial losses, particularly during the early stages of its counteroffensives into Syria and Egypt. In contrast to the Six-Day War, when the Syrian and Egyptian armies collapsed in the face of IDF pressure, they held their positions in the Yom Kippur War, often retreating in good order. This discipline, in tandem with the firepower at their disposal, meant that the IDF paid a high price for its victory in the war.

5

Israeli Resurgence on the Golan versus in the Sinai

In the early afternoon of October 6, 1973, the Syrian and Egyptian armies launched simultaneous offensives against the Israel Defense Forces (IDF) on the Golan and in the Sinai, respectively. Due to a combination of faulty intelligence analysis and poor government decision making, the IDF's reserve forces, which represented the bulk of its fighting power, had not been mobilized and deployed to the fronts in anticipation of these offensives; therefore, Israeli forces on both fronts were heavily outnumbered in tanks, infantry, and artillery at the outset of battle. The lopsided force ratios, combined with the IDF's general physical and psychological unpreparedness for war, allowed the Syrian and Egyptian armies to advance at the outset of the war.

On the Golan front, three infantry divisions, each of which had an independent tank brigade attached to it, backed up by two more tank divisions in the rear, slammed into the Israeli front line. In the northern sector of the Golan, the Syrian army made little headway, stopped in its tracks by the brilliant defensive stand of a single Israeli tank brigade. In the southern sector, on the other hand, the Syrian army penetrated to a depth of 20–25 kilometers before being halted by IDF forces.[1] Nevertheless, by October 7, the second day of the war, the tide on the northern front had already begun to turn in the IDF's favor. By October 10, the IDF had driven the Syrian army back to the prewar cease-fire line and, on October 11, it launched a counteroffensive into Syrian territory that brought it to within artillery range of the Syrian capital's suburbs by October 14.

On the Sinai front, five infantry divisions crossed the Suez Canal and established bridgeheads on the Israeli side of the waterway during the opening phase of the Egyptian offensive. These divisions would later be bolstered by the transfer of tank divisions across the canal.

CHAPTER 5

Though Egyptian forces never penetrated very far into the Sinai—at the their deepest, these bridgeheads extended no more than 10–20 kilometers into Israeli territory—they survived largely intact until the war drew to a close on October 24.[2] While the IDF eventually won the war on the southern front, the tide really did not begin to turn in its favor until October 14, when it crushed the Egyptian army in a massive tank battle.

The IDF, in short, righted itself more quickly on the northern front than on the southern front. Its speedier recovery in the north can be attributed in part to the fact that Israel granted precedence to this front after the first few days of the war. A Central Intelligence Agency (CIA) summary of the Yom Kippur War cogently remarks that:

> Strategically, the Israelis gave first priority to the Syrian front because Arab gains there would have had an immediate adverse effect on Israel even if the Syrians were prevented from occupying any territory inside Israel's pre-1967 [Six-Day War] borders. The prospect of Syrian forces regaining the Golan . . . from which they could resume shelling [northern] Israeli [towns and villages] was intolerable to Israel.[3]

The IDF's quicker turnaround on the northern front, however, cannot be explained solely by Israel's concern about the consequences of a Syrian conquest of the Golan. A number of variables at the tactical and operational levels of warfare also serve to account for the IDF's more rapid recovery on this front. These variables, in no particular order of importance, include: the topography of the Golan and Sinai battlefields; the quantity and quality of IDF forces on the Golan and Sinai front lines at the outbreak of hostilities; the functioning of IDF command and control (C^2) systems on the Golan and in the Sinai; the speed and efficiency of IDF reserve mobilization on both fronts; the application of Israeli airpower on the Golan and in the Sinai; and the extent to which the principles of combined arms warfare were observed by IDF forces on the Golan and in the Sinai.

The Topography of the Golan and Sinai Battlefields

Topographically speaking, the IDF seemed to be in a superior position to defend the Sinai in comparison to the Golan before the Yom Kippur War. To seize part or all of the former, after all, the Egyptian army first had to cross a very formidable water obstacle, the Suez Canal, whereas to seize part or all of the latter, the Syrian army faced no similarly forbidding natural obstacle. The Egyptian army, however, took the Suez Canal out of play as a defensive barrier on the opening day of the war by meticulously crafting and executing its crossing operation. Indeed, the Egyptian army planned and carried out this operation so well that it lost a mere 200–300 men in the effort (as opposed to its prewar estimate of up to 10,000 dead).[4]

The terrain in the Sinai close by the canal is largely flat, sandy, and marshy. The terrain on the Golan, to the contrary, is essentially hilly and rocky. The natural obstacles in the Sinai, therefore, offered much less in the way of high ground and concealment for the heavily outnumbered IDF forces to exploit to their advantage in their defensive stand than the natural obstacles on the Golan provided to their counterparts. To the natural obstacles that favored the Israeli defensive effort on the Golan must also be added the man-made obstacles, which also favored IDF forces in the north over those in the south.

In the Sinai, the IDF constructed the so-called Bar Lev Line—a string of strongpoints along the length of the Suez Canal—in the years before the outbreak of the Yom Kippur War. IDF engineers built a total of more than 30 strongpoints, but half of them had since been closed down for financial and other reasons, so only half were manned on October 6.[5] Most of the active strongpoints were located far apart from each other and, thus, could not offer fire support to each other. Though the strongpoints were surrounded by minefields, and at least some had prepared firing ramps for tanks, they were not intended to withstand a full-scale offensive. Rather, their main purpose was to observe and report the movements of Egyptian forces and to harass those forces that approached them. Finally, IDF engineers constructed a sand wall on the Israeli side of the Suez Canal, but Egyptian army engineers punched holes in it with ease during the crossing operation.[6]

The system of man-made obstacles on the Golan bore a certain resemblance to the system of man-made obstacles in the Sinai, but turned out to be more formidable in practice. An antitank ditch, which the Syrians experienced considerable trouble in crossing, accompanied by extensive minefields, served as a sort of northern, man-made substitute for the Suez Canal.[7] A string of hilltop strongpoints spanning the length of the front backed up the antitank ditch and minefields. Like their counterparts on the Bar Lev Line, these strongpoints were intended mainly to observe and report movements and to harass forces headed toward them; however, their hilltop locations made them much more defensible than their southern counterparts. Finally, especially in the northern sector of the Golan, IDF engineers had prepared an extensive system of firing ramps for tanks, which would prove crucial to the Israeli defense of this portion of the front.

The Quantity and Quality of IDF Forces on the Golan and in the Sinai

The quantity and quality of IDF forces on the Golan and in the Sinai differed in a couple of significant respects at the outset of hostilities. The quality of the tank forces on both fronts was first-rate. On the Sinai front, however, the IDF deployed the equivalent of only one tank brigade—fewer than 100 tanks—in forward positions near the Suez Canal, and some of these tanks were dispersed in small groups to bolster specific Bar Lev Line strongpoints.[8] The IDF deployed two other tank brigades of its standing tank division in the Sinai to the rear, where they could not immediately contest an Egyptian army offensive. On the Golan, in contrast, the IDF deployed almost two tank brigades—about 175 tanks—in forward positions, ready to respond instantly to a Syrian army offensive.[9] Moreover, these tanks remained grouped into battalions and companies instead of being parceled out in small groups.

A second crucial difference concerned the quality of the infantrymen manning the strongpoints on the southern and northern fronts. The Bar Lev Line was garrisoned primarily by low-quality infantrymen who were not really fit physically or psychologically to face an Egyptian offensive and who were either supposed to be replaced or bolstered by elite infantrymen prior to the outbreak of hostilities.[10] Neither IDF general headquarters (GHQ) nor southern command headquarters (HQ), however, ordered the swap or reinforcement to take place in the days before the war. The Golan strongpoints, on the other hand, were garrisoned by parachute and other elite infantrymen who were prepared physically and psychologically to defend against a Syrian offensive.[11]

These quantitative and qualitative differences had a profound effect on how the war initially unfolded in the Sinai and on the Golan. In the Sinai, the Bar Lev Line strongpoints, with a couple of exceptions, proved unable to disrupt the Egyptian crossing.[12] Nor could they fulfill their function of observing and reporting Egyptian movements. And most of them began to call for assistance soon after the commencement of hostilities, as they came under attack by Egyptian forces.

The IDF responded by dispatching tanks in efforts to relieve strongpoints in distress. Unsupported as they were by infantry and artillery—little of either was at the front on the opening day of hostilities—large numbers of these tanks fell prey to Egyptian fire as they advanced to the relief of the strongpoints, especially to antitank missiles and rockets, which could be easily employed over the Sinai's flat terrain. By the second day of the war, the Bar Lev Line was in tatters—all but one strongpoint would either fall or be evacuated within a few days of the commencement of hostilities—and approximately two-thirds of the IDF tank force in the Sinai on October 6 had been put out of action. Furthermore, the Egyptians had established firm bridgeheads all along the length of the Suez Canal.

On the Golan, the Syrian offensive did not progress nearly as smoothly.[13] For starters, with one exception, an intelligence-gathering post on Mount Hermon, Syrian forces did not capture the IDF's hilltop strongpoints. Collectively, not only did they put up stiff resistance to the Syrian offensive, but they also called in effective artillery bombardments and air strikes, particularly on supply convoys following in the wake of the first-echelon attackers. Many of the strongpoints held out until relieved a few days later, while IDF forces evacuated those whose situations had become untenable in a swift and orderly fashion that did not entail significant losses in men and machines.

With its tank brigades unencumbered by the necessity to go to the assistance of the strongpoints, they could concentrate fully on parrying the Syrian offensive. The IDF tank brigade stationed on the northern sector of the front waged a brilliant mobile battle, making excellent use of the terrain and the firing ramps in the area. Consequently, the Syrian offensive made no real headway in this sector, and the Syrian army lost hundreds of tanks, as well as hundreds of armored personnel carriers (APCs), in five days of fighting. The IDF tank brigade stationed on the southern sector of the front had fewer tanks at its disposal and faced a more numerous foe. The Syrian army, therefore, pierced Israeli defenses in this sector and advanced toward Israel proper. Nevertheless, the rearguard skirmishes fought by the organized remnants of this brigade delayed the Syrian advance long enough for Israeli airpower and IDF reserve forces to stabilize this sector of the front before the Syrian army reached Israel.

IDF Command and Control (C^2) Systems on the Golan and in the Sinai

C^2 problems at the operational level in the Sinai compounded the IDF's difficulties at the tactical level. Conversely, the lack of such problems at the operational level on the Golan contributed to the IDF's achievements at the tactical level on this front.[14] Throughout the war, but especially during the first week, IDF forces in the Sinai were plagued by serious C^2 problems stemming from the dysfunctional relationships among IDF GHQ, IDF southern command HQ, and division commanders and their subordinates. Clear lines of communication did not exist at the outset of the war. Nor had specific areas of command responsibility been agreed upon at the outset. Garbled, sometimes contradictory, orders, therefore, were issued by different headquarters (GHQ, southern command HQ, and divisional HQs), frequently based on incomplete and/or inaccurate information as to what was happening in the field, leading to acrimonious exchanges among senior commanders.

Perhaps at no time were these C^2 problems more in evidence than during the IDF's abortive counterattack against the Egyptian bridgeheads on October 8.[15] The plan envisaged a coordinated attack by two reserve tank divisions to roll up the Egyptian bridgeheads from north to south and, perhaps, to capture a bridge across the Suez Canal. In the event, one division launched a couple of disjointed attacks against Egyptian forces, resulting in the destruction of two tank battalions for no tangible gain, while the other division essentially moved around in circles, not taking an active hand in the fighting.

The C^2 situation on the Golan constituted a mirror image of the one in the Sinai. IDF GHQ, IDF northern command HQ, and division commanders and their subordinates worked together as a well-oiled team. Clear lines of communication existed among all HQs, and specific areas of command responsibility were agreed upon early on. Thus, when the first IDF reserve forces deployed to the Golan, they were employed effectively to block the Syrian advance. And, when the IDF began a dedicated counterattack to clear the area of Syrian forces on October 8, after elements of three tank divisions had reached the front, it made steady progress, to the point where the Syrian army was ejected from the whole of the Israeli-controlled portion of the Golan, except from the strongpoint on Mount Hermon, by October 10, allowing Israel to begin a counteroffensive into Syria the next day.

IDF Reserve Mobilization on the Golan and in the Sinai

In the years before the Yom Kippur War, the IDF calculated that it would need at least 24–48 hours to mobilize and deploy its reserve forces to the fronts—and this estimate was based on the assumption that it would be provided with a generous amount of early warning of the commencement of hostilities. Despite the fact that the IDF received only a few hours of early warning, the mobilization and deployment of the reserves in many respects actually proceeded more quickly on both fronts than the prewar estimate, though the process was not without its problems. Stocks of vital equipment at various arms depots throughout Israel could not be found or were in a state of disrepair. Tank and APC crews often had to be cobbled together from scratch. Still, given the chaotic conditions under which the Yom Kippur War began for Israel, the IDF did a very creditable job of mobilizing and deploying its reserve forces.

In the Sinai, not surprisingly, the IDF assigned priority to the mobilization and deployment of tank forces, in part to compensate for losses suffered during the first day of the war. The IDF did not possess enough tank transporters to ferry all of its tanks to the front, so many tanks had to drive all the way from their depots in southern Israel to the western edge of the Sinai on their own tracks. Consequently, many broke down along the way.[16] Furthermore, because the IDF assigned priority to tank forces, the mobilization and deployment of infantry and artillery forces took a back seat. The paucity of infantry and artillery forces would be strongly felt during the abortive October 8 counterattack. Their absence from the battle meant that Egyptian antitank infantrymen had a largely free hand to fire their missiles and rockets at IDF tanks. Without being subjected to suppressive fire, these infantrymen were able to inflict heavy tank losses.

On the Golan, the first IDF reserve forces arrived within 12 hours of the commencement of hostilities.[17] The speedy deployment of reserve forces to this front is not all that surprising in light of the fact that IDF arms depots in northern Israel were not too distant from the Golan. By the end of October 7, substantial elements of three tank divisions were on the plateau, where they were effectively positioned by IDF northern command HQ and divisional commanders to halt the Syrian offensive and to stabilize the front. By October 8, the IDF had amassed enough forces to begin a counterattack, which drove the Syrian army from the Israeli-controlled portion of the Golan by the end of October 10.

Israeli Airpower on the Golan and in the Sinai

In the years prior to the Yom Kippur War, the Israel Air Force (IAF) developed operational plans to destroy Arab integrated air defense systems (IADSs) at the outset of hostilities. The air force contended that it would need 48 hours to complete this task. During this time, according to IAF HQ, IDF ground forces would be not be able to count on air support. Once the IAF had eliminated the Arab IADSs, thereby assuring itself of air superiority over the battlefields, it would engage in a high-tempo air support campaign on behalf of the ground forces.

The IAF preferred to implement its prewar operational plans in the form of a preemptive strike, but the Israeli government refused to sanction this course of action, because it feared that, if the IDF struck the first blow, the United States would abandon Israel to its fate.[18] So, rather than use the few hours of early warning at least to begin to implement its prewar operational plans, the IAF spent the first afternoon and evening of the war defending Israeli territory by shooting down Arab fighter-bombers and troop-carrying helicopters. It flew relatively few air support sorties on either front.

On the morning of the second day of the war, October 7, the IAF began to implement its operational plan to destroy the Egyptian IADS. Known as Challenge 4, the operation made some initial progress, but was soon called off by IDF GHQ as a result of the dire situation on the southern sector of the Golan. The IAF diverted much of its strength to the north. A hasty attempt to execute Model 5, the name of the operational plan to destroy the Syrian IADS, ended in defeat. Even though the Syrian IADS remained intact, the IAF flew many air support sorties on the Golan during the day into the teeth of this system. Many of these sorties hit rear-echelon supply convoys, mauling them and disrupting the Syrian army's advance enough for Israeli reserve forces to reach and to stabilize the front. The IAF's accomplishments here did not come without a steep price, however. It lost 13 fighter-bombers over the Golan on October 7, the most aircraft it lost in a single day over either front.[19]

On every day of the war, except for October 11, the first day of the IDF counteroffensive into Syria, the IAF actually flew more air support sorties on the Sinai front than on the Golan front.[20] And, during the first week of the war, from October 6 to October 12, it lost almost as many aircraft in the Sinai as on the Golan, 35 versus 40 (though not all of the losses, on either front, of course, occurred during air support sorties).[21] Yet, the IAF's air support effort in the Sinai bore less fruit than its effort on the Golan during the first week of the war, and the IAF played less of a role in the IDF's resurgence on this front. Perhaps the principal reason is that its air support sorties were heavily focused on knocking out Egyptian bridges over the Suez Canal, which were hard to hit and easily reparable when they were hit. Moreover, many of the remaining air support sorties were flown in ultimately futile efforts to save beleaguered outposts of the Bar Lev Line.

Combined Arms Warfare on the Golan and in the Sinai

Combined arms warfare refers to the practice of integrating different kinds of forces—tank forces, infantry forces, artillery forces, engineering forces, aerial forces, and so forth—on the battlefield in order to accomplish military objectives.[22] The thinking behind combined arms warfare—and this thinking has been shown to be correct time and again—is that a balanced mix of different kinds of forces offers a better prospect of success on the battlefield than overreliance on one or two types of forces at the expense of the others.

In the years before the Yom Kippur War, the IDF approach to combined arms warfare had become decidedly distorted in favor of tanks and fighter-bombers, especially as a result of the IDF's spectacular victory in the 1967 Six-Day War. The IDF concluded that this war had essentially been won by the actions of the armored corps and the air force. Hence, in the aftermath of the Six-Day War, the IDF not only skewed its force structure heavily in favor of tanks and fighter-bombers, but it also revised its war-fighting doctrine to confer upon them even more prominent roles in its tactical and operational plans. Concomitantly, the IDF reduced its emphasis on infantry, artillery, engineers, and logistics. These forces had to make do with inadequate quantities of men and machines, and the quality of these men and machines often suffered as well. Moreover, the IDF reduced the role of these forces in its war-fighting doctrine at both the tactical and operational levels.

During the first days of the war on the Sinai front, this distorted force structure and war-fighting doctrine had serious consequences. A paucity of mechanized infantry and artillery meant that the IDF engaged in unsupported "tank charges" in the face of well-entrenched Egyptian forces in order to relieve Bar Lev Line strongpoints in distress, leading to heavy losses in tanks, particularly to antitank missiles and rockets. Nor could the IAF act as "flying artillery" in support of the tanks, as had been envisaged in the IDF's prewar thinking, because of the intolerable toll that would have been exacted by the presence of the Egyptian IADS. Had mechanized infantry and artillery been afforded a more prominent role in the IDF's force structure and war-fighting doctrine before the war, perhaps more of these forces would have been on hand to provide suppressive fire against

Egyptian antitank infantry. Likewise, the IDF's abortive October 8 counterattack might have turned out somewhat differently had tanks had adequate support from mechanized infantry and artillery as they advanced toward Egyptian positions.

To its credit, the IDF quickly learned from its initial encounters in the Yom Kippur War, adopting a more traditional approach to combined arms warfare. The tide of the war on the southern front began to turn on October 14, when the IDF destroyed 200–250 Egyptian tanks in a massive battle at a cost of 10–20 of its own tanks.[23] The IDF, not coincidentally, employed traditional combined arms warfare at the operational and tactical levels during this battle. At the operational level, the IAF cooperated with IDF ground forces in halting Egyptian tank thrusts that moved beyond the range of the Egyptian IADS. And, at the tactical level, mechanized infantry and artillery, which had finally been cobbled together in adequate numbers, effectively suppressed Egyptian antitank infantry, so the latter's missiles and rockets played no part in the fighting.[24] From this point forward on the southern front, the IDF would engage in traditional combined arms warfare at the operational and tactical levels, leading to its eventual victory 10 days later.

On the Golan front, the IDF's prewar force structure and warfighting doctrine also caused problems, though they were not as severe as in the Sinai. To help prevent a Syrian breakthrough in the southern Golan, for example, the IAF had to act as flying artillery in the face of an intact Syrian IADS, regardless of the cost to itself, because the IDF did not possess sufficient artillery strength. On the other hand, tanks could function much more easily with minimal or no infantry and artillery support on the Golan than in the Sinai, because the hilly and rocky terrain prevented the Syrian army from deploying its antitank missiles and rockets, whose effective use depended on clear lines of sight.[25] Moreover, the smooth command relationships and the high quality of all forces on the Golan created conditions for the early adoption of traditional combined arms warfare at both the operational and tactical levels. Thus, for example, the elite infantrymen in the hilltop strongpoints acted as efficient forward observers calling in artillery bombardments and air strikes against vulnerable Syrian rear-echelon supply columns.

Summary

The IDF won the Yom Kippur War on the northern front before the tide had even turned in its favor on the southern front. This fact cannot be explained entirely by the strategic choice at the beginning of the war to give preference to the former, because of its proximity to Israel proper. The combined effects of six variables worked to the IDF's advantage on the Golan versus the Sinai early on in the war. The interaction of terrain obstacles (natural and man-made), the quantity and quality of forces on the front lines, the performance of C^2, the smoothness of reserve mobilization, the application of airpower, and the practice of combined arms warfare made possible the IDF's stout defensive stand on the Golan and hindered its defensive stand in the Sinai. Had these six variables complemented each other as well in the south as in the north during the early days of the war, the IDF would undoubtedly have won a swifter and less costly victory here.

6

Israeli Airpower in the Six-Day and Yom Kippur Wars

The 1967 Six-Day War and the 1973 Yom Kippur War began quite differently for the Israel Air Force (IAF).[1] During the opening day of the Six-Day War, on the basis of a meticulously planned and exhaustively rehearsed operational plan, which it refined and updated in the three weeks prior to the outbreak of hostilities, the IAF assumed the initiative against the air forces of Egypt, Jordan, and Syria, taking them by surprise on the ground. The first few days of the Yom Kippur War, to the contrary, found the IAF scrambling to respond to an Egyptian–Syrian surprise attack against Israel. Though the IAF had carefully planned and thoroughly rehearsed operational plans, in this instance aimed primarily at Arab integrated air defense systems (IADSs) rather than at Arab air forces, the diplomatic and military circumstances prior to the onset of hostilities prevented it from seizing the initiative.

The conditions prevailing at the outset of each war determined the IAF's performance in the opening phases of these conflicts. In the Six-Day War, the IAF essentially annihilated the combined Arab air forces of Egypt, Jordan, and Syria in a few hours by launching several waves of highly coordinated air base attacks. The virtually complete elimination of Arab airpower—and the concomitant early achievement of air superiority over the battlefields—then left it free to concentrate on other roles in support of the Israeli war effort. During the Yom Kippur War, on the other hand, the IAF did not have the opportunity to secure air superiority over the battlefields early in the conflict, because the Israel Defense Forces (IDF) general headquarters (GHQ) insisted that it fly close air support (CAS) and interdiction sorties on behalf of hard-pressed ground forces. With sustained operations against Arab IADSs not an option—and with these systems subjected only to intermittent and hesitant IAF strikes—they exacted a significant toll on Israeli

CHAPTER 6

aircraft at modest cost to themselves during the first few days of the war.

The immense victory scored by the IAF against the Arab air forces during the Six-Day War, followed by the equally impressive triumph registered by IDF ground forces against the Egyptian, Jordanian, and Syrian armies, creates the distinct impression that airpower played an overwhelming role in that victory. Contrariwise, the early setback suffered by the IAF at the hands of Arab IADSs during the Yom Kippur War, coupled with the much longer period of time that it took the IDF to defeat the Egyptian and Syrian armies in comparison to the Six-Day War (almost three weeks versus less than one), creates the distinct impression that airpower did not make a major contribution to the Israeli victory.

Admittedly, these impressions seem valid upon first reflection. With Arab air forces quickly eliminated as a threat both to Israel proper and to IDF ground forces, the IAF participated extensively in the ground battles on the Sinai (Egyptian), Judean and Samarian (Jordanian), and Golan (Syrian) fronts during the Six-Day War, inflicting substantial damage on Arab armies on particular occasions. The long lines of burned out Egyptian army vehicles in and around the Sinai passes serve as mute testimony to this fact. The IAF's inability in the Yom Kippur War to neutralize the Egyptian and Syrian IADSs, especially in the early phase of the conflict, hindered its capacity to support the IDF's ground forces. That the Egyptian army could move tens of thousands of troops and thousands of vehicles across the Suez Canal during the first days of the war with only minor losses caused by the IAF serves as eloquent testimony to this fact.

A careful examination of the relative contributions of Israeli airpower to the 1967 and 1973 war efforts, however, reveals a far less clear-cut, much more complex tapestry. Though its significant contribution to the IDF's victory in the Six-Day War is undeniable, the IAF did not win the war for Israel. Nor can the IAF's performance in the Yom Kippur War be deemed the principal reason why it took the IDF so long to defeat its Arab opponents. Its initial problems with Arab IADSs notwithstanding, the IAF played a rather substantial role in the IDF's eventual triumph.

Perhaps the best means with which to gauge the actual contributions of Israeli airpower to the Israeli war efforts in the 1967 and 1973 wars is to compare the IAF's performance in each of its four main combat roles—air superiority, CAS, interdiction, and strategic attack—as well as in each of its four ancillary, "noncombat" roles—troop transport, casualty evacuation, logistical support, and reconnaissance—across both wars.² But it is first necessary to define each of these roles in general terms, as well as to describe in broad strokes the IAF's accomplishments (or lack thereof) in each war, so that its relative performance can be judged accordingly.

General Definitions of Combat and Noncombat Roles

An air force that has achieved air superiority in a conflict is one that essentially controls the skies over the theater of operations. Such an air force is able to carry out all of its assigned roles—for example, CAS and interdiction—secure in the knowledge that its aircraft face only minimal opposition from an opponent's air force and IADS. Such an air force is also able to deny its opponent's air force the capability to fulfill these same roles by ensuring that enemy aircraft cannot survive in sufficient numbers to be effective.

Air supremacy is an extreme form of air superiority. An air force that has obtained air supremacy over the theater of operations is one that has gained virtually unchallenged command of the skies such that its own aircraft can complete their assignments at almost no risk to themselves and such that its opponent's aircraft stand almost no chance of survival, let alone of executing their assignments.

Both CAS and interdiction involve attacks on an opponent's ground forces (or other targets) situated on the battlefield. The distinction between these roles is the proximity of the attacks to friendly ground forces. CAS involves attacks against an opponent's ground forces (or other targets) in very close proximity to friendly forces. It requires precise coordination between air and ground forces to assure the avoidance of "fratricide." Interdiction, in contrast, involves attacks against an opponent's ground forces (or other targets), which, while on the battlefield, are not in very close proximity to friendly forces. This type of sortie does not require the same high level of air–land coordination, as the prospect of fratricide is not a consideration.

Strategic attack sorties are directed against military or nonmilitary (but war-related) targets—for example, central headquarters (HQs); munitions depots; petroleum, oil, and lubricants (POL) storage dumps; and port facilities—that are not typically located on the battlefield itself, but rather are generally situated in an opponent's hinterland. These attacks are often characterized, in other words, by the "deep penetration" of an opponent's airspace, and they are intended to serve some strategic objective in a war.³

The four ancillary roles can be defined more succinctly. Troop transport concerns the movement of ground forces to, from, and around the battlefield. Casualty evacuation involves the removal of the wounded from the battlefield. Logistical support concerns the supply of ground forces with consumables, such as vehicles, munitions, POL, food, and water. And, finally, reconnaissance involves data collection with respect to the location and strength of the opponent's forces and targets, on or off of the battlefield, and with respect to damage assessment of forces and targets engaged previously.

A Summary of IAF Activity in the Six-Day War

Following three weeks of fruitless diplomacy to resolve an Arab–Israeli crisis that had erupted as a consequence of border tensions between Israel and Syria, the Israeli government gave the IDF a green light to commence operations against the Egyptian armed forces on the morning of June 5, 1967. The IAF immediately launched Operation Focus, a full-scale preemptive strike on the Egyptian air force that had been planned and practiced for years.[4]

Attacking at an unusual time—well after dawn—and from an unexpected direction—largely from west to east—the IAF caught the Egyptian air force completely unprepared for battle. In a multiwave assault that employed nearly its entire inventory, the IAF continually struck 18 air bases in the Sinai and in Egypt proper throughout June 5 according to a predetermined ranking of targets that gave priority to the destruction of long-range bombers and front-line interceptors. Moreover, the air bases themselves were thoroughly worked over in repeated bombing and strafing runs, and the IAF also struck some of Egypt's radar stations.[5]

Operation Focus devastated the Egyptian air force. Israeli figures record the destruction of approximately 300 aircraft, including the entire long-range bomber fleet and most of the front-line interceptor fleet. Many of the air bases were rendered more or less inoperative, because IAF aircraft had cratered their runways and demolished their facilities, and the Egyptian air force possessed only a rudimentary repair capability. The Egyptian air force, in sum, had been reduced to a mere shadow of its former self in terms of aircraft, air bases, and command and control (C^2) infrastructure.[6]

The Syrian, Jordanian, and Iraqi air forces responded to the IAF's assault on the Egyptian air force by initiating a number of small-scale air attacks against Israel. These strikes caused no appreciable damage, but they did alert the IAF to the potential threat posed by these air forces. The IAF, therefore, embarked on a concerted campaign of air base attacks against them. It promptly and repeatedly struck eight air bases in Syria, Jordan, and Iraq as part of Operation Focus.

The results were much the same as those registered in the Egyptian portion of the operation, though on a considerably smaller scale. The IAF destroyed about half of the Syrian air force, including many of its front-line interceptors. Jordan lost almost all of its combat aircraft, and Iraq lost a number of planes. All together, the IAF destroyed about 90 Syrian, Jordanian, and Iraqi aircraft. Air bases were again pummeled to the point where they became unserviceable, with runways cratered and facilities smashed beyond easy repair.[7]

While Operation Focus exacted a considerable toll on the IAF, which lost 18 of the approximately 250 combat aircraft (including armed trainers) in its prewar inventory, it was now largely free to support IDF ground forces.[8] The IAF's CAS and interdiction effort got underway in earnest on the second day of the war. Of the 2,591 CAS and interdiction sorties flown by the IAF throughout the war, a mere 268 occurred on the first day.[9] Most of the ground attack sorties throughout the war were interdiction strikes, as the IAF had neither the C^2 infrastructure nor an adequate number of the proper type of aircraft (i.e., low- and slow-flying straight-winged platforms) to engage in a high-tempo CAS effort in close coordination with advancing IDF ground forces.

On the Sinai front, the IAF typically launched strikes far in the Egyptian rear, gradually working its way back toward an ever-shifting front line.[10] Most of the damage inflicted on the Egyptian army by air attack occurred during its panic-stricken retreat through the Sinai mountain passes toward the Suez Canal on the third and fourth days of the war. And most of the vehicles destroyed by the IAF were "soft" targets, such as trucks and jeeps, which composed the Egyptian army's logistical "tail." Relatively few tanks and other armored fighting vehicles were knocked out by Israeli airpower.[11] The IAF, in other words, did not cause heavy damage to the Egyptian army's front-line units and operational reserves, the "teeth" that engaged the IDF's ground forces.

The Judean and Samarian front witnessed a similar story, even if the IAF "softened up" this front for the IDF's ground forces to a greater extent at the outset of the fighting. The IAF placed much of its emphasis on interdiction strikes against logistical and infrastructure targets located in the Jordanian army's rear. While the IAF did not pin down or obliterate the army's front-line forces, it did scatter or stall at least some units from the operational reserves rushing to the front line, and it did inflict substantial damage on other units retreating back toward Jordan proper. And the IAF also prevented an Iraqi expeditionary force from reaching the front. While the IAF most likely had a somewhat greater impact on the ground battles in Judea and Samaria than in the Sinai, it by no means compromised the fighting ability of the Jordanian army.

The situation on the Golan front differed from those on the Sinai and Judean and Samarian fronts in that the IAF flew hundreds of interdiction sorties in the days prior to the commencement of the IDF ground assault against the Syrian army. These air attacks had a negligible effect on the heavily bunkered defensive positions on the Golan—IAF munitions of the late 1960s could not penetrate them—so the impact on the Syrian army's front-line units turned out to be principally psychological in nature. Interdiction strikes, on the other hand, did disrupt road traffic, inhibiting the capacity of the operational reserves to bolster the front-line positions. Airpower, though, again made itself felt most intensely during the retreat phase of the fighting.

A rather small air force (by major power standards) in 1967, the IAF consequently sought to maximize the number of combat aircraft in its inventory. Hence, its transport and helicopter fleets got the short end of the stick. Yet, the IAF did possess enough assets in these areas to fulfill ancillary roles. It transported paratroopers behind Egyptian lines on at least three occasions and behind Syrian lines on at least one occasion.[12] The IAF also removed wounded soldiers from the battlefields on all three fronts. Logistically speaking, fuel drops allowed a number of hard-charging IDF armored columns to continue virtually uninterrupted their advance toward the Suez Canal.[13] And, finally, the air force carried out regular reconnaissance flights, with combat aircraft serving in a dual role, for both battle-damage-assessment and target-location purposes on all fronts.

A Summary of IAF Activity in the Yom Kippur War

Unlike the Six-Day War, when the IDF had three weeks in which to mobilize and deploy for war, the Yom Kippur War caught Israel by surprise. The IDF's ground forces, particularly the reserve armored divisions that made up the bulk of its fighting power, were neither mobilized nor deployed along the Sinai and Golan fronts. The IAF, on the other hand, which has always been much less dependent on reserve manpower than the ground forces, had enough advanced warning of the impending Egyptian and Syrian assault to launch a preemptive strike. Ideally, the IAF wanted to be given two days of advanced warning to prepare to implement Operation Challenge 4 (Sinai front) and/or Operation Model 5 (Golan front), but it did possess the capability to execute either one with just a few hours of preparation. The IAF also had a more modest plan—one that could also be executed after just a few hours of preparation—known as Operation Ram, a contingency plan that focused on the destruction of Syrian air bases. Under intense American pressure, however, the Israeli government refused to sanction any preemptive strike.[14] The IDF had to absorb the first blow in this war.

Consequently, contrary to its preference, the IAF never got a genuine opportunity to implement its intricate prewar operational plans to launch massive coordinated attacks against both the Egyptian and Syrian IADSs, which it perceived to be the major obstacles to the attainment of air superiority over the Sinai and Golan battlefields. The IAF did attempt to implement Operation Challenge 4 on the second day of hostilities, meeting with initial success, but IDF GHQ quickly canceled the operation in order to divert the IAF's full strength to the Golan front in an effort to prevent a potential Syrian armored breakthrough into Israel proper.[15] Instead the IAF had to make do throughout the war with hastily improvised, piecemeal attacks against both IADSs at times when it had resources available for this task.

Not surprisingly, then, the results of its attacks against the Egyptian and Syrian IADSs proved to be decidedly mixed. On the Sinai front, in a series of combined operations with IDF ground forces that had crossed to the Egyptian side of the Suez Canal, the IAF eventually managed to pierce the Egyptian IADS, destroying about one third of its surface-to-air missile (SAM) batteries, opening up undefended flight corridors, but only during the final phase of the war.[16] On the Golan front, in contrast, the IAF could not punch holes in the Syrian IADS, though it thinned out the number of SAM batteries stationed at the front. Emblematic of the IAF's troubles on this front, a much scaled-down and very short-lived version of Operation Model 5, also executed on the second day of the war, resulted in the loss of six aircraft without causing appreciable damage to the Syrian IADS. Not only was this operation based on outdated and inaccurate intelligence, but it was also very poorly coordinated: most of the electronic countermeasures (ECM) systems (mounted in helicopters), which were intended to jam Syrian fire-control radars, were not available during the attack; the unmanned aerial vehicles (UAVs) that were supposed to serve as decoys in order to mask the IAF's strike aircraft during the attack were fired off too early in the operation to play their role; and the long-range artillery bombardment that was supposed to accompany the air attack

CHAPTER 6

never took place. At war's end, less than 15 percent of Syria's SAM batteries had been destroyed by the IAF.[17]

If the IAF had a rough time with the Egyptian and Syrian IADSs, which accounted for the majority of the approximately 105–110 Israeli aircraft (including helicopters) lost throughout the war, the same cannot be said of its encounter with the Egyptian and Syrian air forces.[18] It shot down approximately 275–300 Arab aircraft in air-to-air combat for the loss of perhaps 15–20 of its own.[19] Whatever the precise number of losses on each side, the IAF reigned supreme in air battles throughout the war, even on the first day of the fighting, when it not only downed many Egyptian fighter-bombers, but also a substantial number of troop-carrying helicopters trying to drop Egyptian special operations forces behind Israeli lines.

Moreover, the IAF flew hundreds of air base attack sorties during the war, mainly against Egyptian airfields, despite knowing that these sorties would destroy only a handful of aircraft on the ground and would close down only a handful of air bases for short periods of time (because Arab air forces had hardened their facilities and improved their repair capabilities after the Six-Day War debacle).[20] It flew these sorties primarily in order to keep both the Egyptian and Syrian air forces and IADSs on the defensive.

Of the more than 11,200 sorties flown by Israeli aircraft during the Yom Kippur War, approximately 7,300 (or about two-thirds) were devoted to CAS or interdiction.[21] Because the IDF's ground forces were not ready to counter the Egyptian–Syrian surprise attack, the IAF had to operate as "flying artillery" during the opening days of the war in order to "fill the gaps in Israeli defensive positions," especially on the Golan front.[22] Rather than begin a dedicated CAS and interdiction campaign after delivering a sharp blow to Arab IADSs, as called for in its prewar operational plans, the IAF had to conduct this campaign throughout the war, often in the face of intense ground fire.

On the Sinai front, the IAF initially concentrated its CAS strikes around the besieged IDF strongholds on the Bar Lev Line and its interdiction strikes against the Egyptian bridgeheads over the Suez Canal.[23] Though the IAF hit a number of the bridges that spanned the canal, the Egyptians proved able to repair them very quickly. Once the IAF's focus switched to the Golan front, it reduced the number of CAS and interdiction strikes on the Sinai front, especially in light of its heavy losses to the Arab IADSs during the first few days of hostilities.[24] Until IDF ground forces counterattacked across the Suez Canal and began to demolish SAM batteries on the Egyptian side of the canal, the IAF's CAS and interdiction effort concentrated almost exclusively on

1 Before the Yom Kippur War, the Israeli defense establishment assumed – incorrectly, in the event – that the might of the Israel Air Force (IAF) would deter Israel's Arab foes from launching a war.

2 Israeli tanks and mechanized infantry generally fought well together as part of combined arms task forces on the Golan front.

3 A lack of coordination between Israeli aircraft and ground forces constituted a serious problem throughout most of the Yom Kippur War.

4 A shortage of artillery hampered Israeli forces during the Yom Kippur War, especially on the Sinai front.

5 Unsupported Israeli "tank charges" during the early days of hostilities on the Sinai front resulted in heavy armor losses.

6 Israeli forces on the Sinai front suffered heavily in the first days of the war, partly as a consequence of poor command and control (C^2).

7 Israeli fighter-bombers coped very well with Egyptian and Syrian aircraft, but performed far less efficiently against Egyptian and Syrian air defense systems.

8 The creation of an Israeli bridgehead across the Suez Canal constituted a turning point on the Sinai front during the Yom Kippur War.

9 Once Israeli forces crossed over the Suez Canal, they destroyed or captured many Egyptian surface-to-air missile (SAM) emplacements.

10 The excellent performance of the Israel Navy (IN) during the war convinced the Israeli defense establishment that it could undertake additional responsibilities in future rounds of hostilities.

11 The Israeli government asked the members of the Agranat Commission to uncover the reasons why the Israel Defense Forces (IDF) had been unprepared for battle on the eve of the Yom Kippur War, as well as the reasons why Israeli forces had experienced setbacks in the opening days of hostilities.

Egyptian forces operating outside of their air defense umbrella. Only in the last phase of the war, with the penetration of the system, did the IAF intensify its CAS and interdiction effort on this front, in order to support the IDF's counteroffensive into Egypt.

Out of necessity, the IAF operated according to a somewhat different set of rules on the Golan front. Because IDF GHQ feared a Syrian armored breakthrough into Israel proper during the first days of the war, the IAF had to engage in a grinding CAS and interdiction effort on this front at the outset of the war, regardless of the cost to itself. Only after the mobilization and deployment of the IDF's reserve armored divisions allowed the IDF to clear the Golan of the Syrian army and then to launch a successful counteroffensive into Syria proper did the IAF's effort slacken in intensity in order to conserve aircraft.

Like the results of its campaign against Arab IADSs, the IAF's CAS and interdiction effort yielded decidedly mixed results. Notwithstanding the tremendous growth in the firepower of the IAF between the 1967 and 1973 wars, its ability to destroy tanks and other armored fighting vehicles remained quite modest.[25] It possessed neither the required C^2 infrastructure nor the required munitions to be very effective in this regard. Still, the "shock effect" of CAS and interdiction strikes sometimes served to stall or scatter Arab front-line and operational reserve units on both fronts.

The IAF, as in the Six-Day War, had much more of an impact against thin-skinned logistical vehicles. Indeed, on the Golan front, IAF attacks on supply convoys disrupted the Syrian offensive, giving IDF ground forces valuable extra time to mobilize and deploy for defense. On the Sinai front, IAF attacks on supply convoys contributed to the Egyptian Third Army's inability to prevent IDF ground forces from surrounding and besieging it at the end of the war.

In contrast to the Six-Day War, the IAF conducted a series of strategic attacks in the Yom Kippur War, albeit of limited scope and duration. In response to Syrian medium-range rocket attacks against civilian and military targets in northern Israel, the IAF carried out at least one bombing raid on the Syrian capital, Damascus, causing damage to both the defense ministry complex and air force headquarters. It also pulverized POL storage and port facilities deep within Syria.

Between 1967 and 1973, the IAF upgraded its transport and helicopter fleets, thereby increasing its capabilities in the troop transport, casualty evacuation, and logistical support roles. During the Yom Kippur War, it employed helicopters to carry troops to the battlefield on a number of occasions, perhaps most notably during the last phase of the war on the Golan front, when they landed paratroopers and special operations forces on Mount Hermon in order to retake an Israeli intelligence-gathering post that had been overrun early in the war. Helicopters also evacuated thousands of wounded soldiers from the battlefields over the course of the fighting. IAF transport aircraft not only brought munitions directly from the United States to Israel, but they also ferried supplies to the battlefields, particularly after IDF ground forces captured airfields on the Egyptian side of the Suez Canal.

The IAF also upgraded its reconnaissance assets in the interwar period. During the 1973 war, it used both dual-role combat aircraft and helicopters to gather intelligence. It employed the latter mainly to monitor Egyptian and Syrian SAM batteries, while it used the former to carry out battle-damage assessments and to collect information on troop movements and rear-area targets.

A Comparative Assessment of Israeli Airpower in the 1967 and 1973 Wars

In both the 1967 and 1973 wars, the IAF achieved air supremacy over Israel proper. Very few Arab aircraft penetrated Israeli airspace in either conflict, and none of them inflicted any real damage on rear-area targets. An Egyptian attempt to attack the Israeli defense ministry complex in downtown Tel Aviv with air-to-surface missiles during the Yom Kippur War also ended in total failure.[26] The small number of medium-range rockets that Syria fired into northern Israel in this war caused more damage than Egyptian and Syrian air attacks during the conflict.

The attainment of air supremacy over Israel constitutes the most impressive contribution made by the IAF to both Israeli victories. In the Six-Day War, neither Israel's civilian populace nor its industrial assets came under air attack. Had the Arab air forces not been destroyed at the outset of the war, they might have been able to cause considerable damage inside Israel's borders before the termination of hostilities. In the Yom Kippur War, air supremacy was even more important to Israel's triumph. First, Israel's civilian populace and industrial assets were again spared from death and destruction. Second, because the IDF's ground forces had not been mobilized and deployed along the fronts weeks before the outbreak of hostilities, air supremacy over Israel furnished them with the crucial 48 hours of breathing space that they needed to mobilize and deploy fully to the fronts. Had Arab aircraft been able to penetrate Israeli airspace, they might have been able to disrupt the Israeli mobilization effort by attacking key staging areas, which in turn might well have changed the complexion of the war.

In both the 1967 and 1973 wars, the IAF achieved air superiority over the battlefields. In the Six-Day War, the early destruction of Arab air forces—and the consequent air superiority enjoyed by the IAF—not only allowed the air force to begin a dedicated CAS and interdiction campaign on the second day of the war essentially free of concern about interception, but it also meant that IDF ground forces never came under effective air attack throughout the fighting. The few CAS and interdiction sorties flown by surviving Arab aircraft merely pricked IDF ground forces; these sorties in no way impaired the IDF's offensives in the Sinai, in Judea and Samaria, or on the Golan.

The air superiority story in the Yom Kippur War is far more complex. From day one of the war, the IAF achieved air superiority vis-à-vis the Egyptian and Syrian air forces. While it is certainly true that these air forces were far more active throughout the war than they were in 1967, it is equally true that they inflicted only minor damage on IDF ground forces throughout the fighting. Even on the first day—when the Egyptian and Syrian air forces launched their most intense CAS and interdiction strikes of the war—they achieved only meager results, as the IAF effectively disrupted their attacks. The impact of these air forces on the battlefields went downhill from here, and no evidence exists to support the notion that either air force inhibited IDF defensive or offensive operations later in the war. Furthermore, neither the Egyptian nor the Syrian air force was able to prevent the IAF from engaging in CAS or interdiction strikes at any stage of the fighting.

The Egyptian and Syrian IADSs, though, did seriously impair the IAF's CAS and interdiction campaigns on the Sinai and Golan fronts. Though the IAF achieved a rather tenuous air superiority vis-à-vis the Egyptian IADS by the end of the war, it nevertheless still had far from a free hand over the battlefield; and it had even less success against the Syrian IADS, despite the fact that this network also had been thinned out by the end of the war.

Indeed, the most important accomplishment of the IAF with respect to Arab IADSs did not occur on the battlefields themselves, but rather took place in the realm of deterrence. The obsessive fear of Israeli airpower on the part of Egyptian and Syrian military planners encouraged them to load down their armies with antiaircraft defense units at the expense of additional armored and infantry formations. Moreover, these planners limited the scope and pace of the initial offensives on both fronts such that Arab ground forces would not advance beyond the range of their slow-moving IADSs. The Egyptian penetration of the Sinai did not exceed 10–20 kilometers, while the Syrians did not get much further on the Golan. The skewed force structure of Arab ground forces, the limited scope of their opening offensives, and the slow pace at which they advanced at the outbreak of the war all contributed significantly to the IDF's ability to block them from moving further into the Sinai or into northern Israel itself.[27]

The attainment of air superiority over the 1967 and 1973 battlefields also constitutes a very impressive contribution to Israel's triumphs. While the IDF, because of its indisputable qualitative superiority over Arab armies, would most likely have won both wars even had the IAF not achieved air superiority, the fighting, particularly in the Yom Kippur War, would almost certainly have taken a much heavier toll on it.

The IAF's own CAS and interdiction campaigns in both wars played much smaller roles in Israel's victories.[28] In the Six-Day War, IDF ground forces won the all-important "break-in" battles—that is, the first battles of its offensives, the ones that ultimately decided the outcome of the fighting—on the Sinai and the Judean and Samarian fronts with little or no direct assistance from the IAF. When given a choice to fight with airpower during the day or to fight without it at night, IDF division commanders preferred the second option.[29] Even on the Golan front, where the IAF softened up the battlefield for days before the ground assault, the IDF triumphed over the Syrian army mainly because its ground forces ousted the Syrians from their stout defensive positions in a grueling slugging match. The IAF CAS and interdiction campaign, however, by compounding Arab confusion and panic and by inflicting substantial damage on soft targets, did lead to a swifter and more crushing Israeli victory in the war than would otherwise have been the case.

During the Yom Kippur War, the IAF's CAS and interdiction campaign also produced limited results. Its most notable contribution to the Israeli victory occurred on the Golan front, where it helped to stem the Syrian offensive. Nevertheless, credit for the IDF's ultimately successful "blocking" battles on both the Sinai and Golan fronts belongs primarily to the regular and reserve armored forces that fought the Egyptian and Syrian armies to a standstill, despite being heavily outnumbered in both arenas. Likewise, credit for the IDF's successful counteroffensives in the Sinai and on the Golan again belongs mainly to the ground forces. CAS and interdiction strikes hammered some

Egyptian and Syrian front-line and operational reserve units that wandered outside the umbrella of their IADSs, but these strikes did not alter the course of the ground war.

A contrast is often drawn between the allegedly devastating IAF CAS and interdiction campaign in 1967 versus the allegedly anemic campaign in 1973.[30] But a close examination of the results of these campaigns—in terms of the amount of physical destruction visited upon the Egyptian and Syrian armies, though not necessarily in terms of the amount of psychological devastation inflicted on them—reveals that the difference between the two is not all that large. The IAF proved unable to destroy significant numbers of tanks and other armored vehicles in either war. While the shocking scenes of mangled convoys, so prevalent in the Six-Day War, may not have been evident in the Yom Kippur War, the IAF appears to have been equally successful at knocking out soft and rear-echelon targets in both conflicts. And aircraft losses in these campaigns were comparable when adjusted for the numbers of CAS and interdiction sorties flown in each war.[31] Whether the CAS and interdiction campaign could have made a much larger contribution to the Israeli war effort during the Yom Kippur War had the IAF been afforded the opportunity to deal first with Arab IADSs must remain an open question.[32]

The IAF's strategic attacks against Syria during the Yom Kippur War had only a marginal impact on the Israeli war effort. Though the strikes themselves caused substantial damage to infrastructure targets in the Syrian hinterland, they did not detract from Syria's overall warmaking capacity, perhaps because of their restricted scope. They did, however, reinforce Israeli deterrence with respect to the home front, as the Syrians refrained from launching any further rocket attacks into northern Israel once the IAF began to hit rear-area targets. Furthermore, strategic attacks served to thin out Syria's IADS on the Golan, as the Syrian army had to move antiaircraft defense formations to the rear in order to guard sensitive infrastructure targets. This redeployment, in turn, made it easier for IAF aircraft to fly CAS and interdiction sorties.

In terms of its ancillary roles, the IAF had about the same limited impact on the Israeli war effort in both the 1967 and 1973 wars. Troop transport to, from, and around the battlefields was confined almost exclusively to the insertion of paratroopers and special operations forces behind Arab lines. With one or two exceptions in each war, these drops did not play a major part in ground force operations. Casualty evacuation turned out to be a much more significant use of the IAF's airlift capability, probably saving scores of lives in each war. Likewise,

CHAPTER 6

logistical support in the form of IAF-delivered supplies proved important at specific points during both wars. Finally, while the IAF possessed high-quality reconnaissance aircraft, the information collected by these platforms proved to be of scant value to the IDF in both wars, because this data could not be processed and distributed to the relevant commands in real time.[33]

Summary

That the IAF made substantial contributions to Israel's victories in both the 1967 and 1973 wars is not in doubt. Most importantly, it ensured that Israel would not lose either war, which was—and still is—crucial to a state whose opponents contested—and still contest—its very right to exist. The IAF's contributions to Israel's victories with respect to its direct impact on the 1967 and 1973 battlefields in support of the IDF's ground forces, on the other hand, were more modest in scope.

The attainment of air supremacy over Israel proper, as well as the attainment of air superiority over the battlefields, not only spared the state's civilian populace and industrial assets, but also cleared the air, so to speak, for the IDF's ground forces to come to grips with their Arab counterparts. Indeed, because of the radically different set of circumstances under which the IDF began the 1967 and 1973 wars, the IAF actually played a more important part in the latter victory, in the sense that it provided the crucial time and space for the IDF's ground forces to mobilize and deploy for battle. In the words of the IAF commander during the Yom Kippur War:

> Air superiority enabled our forces to mobilize, move[,] and act with no meaningful interference from enemy air. This is something not to be scoffed at under the situation we were in at the beginning [of the war].[34]

The IDF's ground forces, not the IAF, however, ultimately defeated the Arab armies in both wars.

The most fundamental conclusion to be drawn from the IAF's experiences in the 1967 and 1973 wars is that airpower cannot be relied upon to be decisive on the conventional battlefield. If more proof is necessary, one need look no further than Israel's two most inconclusive wars. The 1969–70 War of Attrition and the 2006 Second Lebanon War are the two conflicts in which it relied most heavily on airpower to accomplish its wartime objectives. Even though the IAF performed very well in both wars, the absence of "boots on the ground" in Egypt and Lebanon, respectively, allowed Israel's opponents to escape crushing defeats.

Part III
Lessons

By wise counsel you can wage your war.
Proverbs 24:6

7

The Impact of American Arms Transfers to Israel

In reference to the American arms pipeline to the Israel Defense Forces (IDF) during the 1973 Yom Kippur War, President Anwar Sadat reportedly said that Egypt could not simultaneously fight both Israel and the United States.[1] He no doubt made this remark primarily to pave the way for Egypt to accept a cease-fire with Israel without losing face before the complete collapse of the Egyptian army as a result of the IDF counteroffensive across the Suez Canal. While Sadat's statement cannot be taken as a serious reflection on the military situation obtaining during the Yom Kippur War—the United States, after all, had not entered the war on Israel's behalf and was simply matching Soviet military assistance to Egypt and Syria—it does nevertheless suggest a number of intriguing questions. To what extent did American arms transfers assist the IDF war effort? Did the arms pipeline contribute to Israel's victory over the Syrian army on the Golan front? Did arms transfers contribute to its triumph over the Egyptian army on the Sinai front? Or was the arms pipeline of more political and psychological than military value to Israel during the Yom Kippur War?

Research into the war has thus far not squarely addressed these sorts of questions. The present chapter, therefore, constitutes an initial effort to do so. The first order of business is to lay out the basic facts surrounding the American arms pipeline to Israel. The second order of business is then to describe the major developments on the Golan and Sinai fronts, with a view to determining what, if any, impact American arms transfers during the war had on IDF operations on the northern and southern battlefields.

CHAPTER 7

The Arms Pipeline

Though the Yom Kippur War caught the IDF by surprise, with most of its ground forces nowhere near the front lines, Israel did receive enough early warning of the impending Arab attack—a few hours—to launch a preemptive strike against its opponents' armed forces with its air force; however, Israel did not launch such a strike, largely because it feared that it would get no assistance from the United States during the war if the IDF struck the initial blow.[2] In return for forfeiting this potentially critical military advantage, Israel naturally expected the United States to meet the IDF's arms requests during the war. Thus, immediately upon the outbreak of fighting, Israel asked the United States to supply the IDF with substantial quantities of aircraft, tanks, various types of ammunition and electronic systems, and other items.[3]

For its part, the United States sought to manipulate arms transfers to Israel throughout the war in order to advance a diplomatic agenda intent upon enhancing American influence in the Middle East at the expense of the Soviet Union.[4] Such an agenda, reasoned American officials, would be best served by a limited Israeli victory—that is, a victory against Syria and a stalemate against Egypt—followed by American-brokered talks to resolve the Arab–Israeli conflict. A crushing Israeli victory, concluded these officials, would undercut American efforts to negotiate an end to the conflict.

Consequently, from October 6 through October 12, the first week of the war, the United States essentially deflected Israel's requests for "hardware," like aircraft and tanks, but approved, albeit somewhat grudgingly, small-scale deliveries of "consumables," like certain types of ammunition, especially once it became evident that the IDF would not rout its Arab opponents as it had in the 1967 Six-Day War.[5] Most of these consumables, however, did not reach the IDF in a timely manner. Private sector airline companies in the United States refused to transport munitions to Israel, and bureaucratic infighting between State and Defense Department officials further plugged the arms pipeline.[6] The only American arms received by the IDF during the early part of the war were those brought to Israel by a handful of El Al cargo flights.

The American policy of restraint ended abruptly on October 13, when President Richard Nixon personally authorized a massive airlift—later augmented by a sealift—of arms to Israel.[7] The American change of heart came about mainly as a result of a massive Soviet air- and sealift of arms to Egypt and Syria, which had begun as early as October 8, coupled with an Arab–Soviet refusal to consider a cease-fire arrangement. The United States concluded that it simply could not leave its client in the lurch while the Soviet Union violated its commitments under détente and unreservedly backed its Arab clients. To have done so would not only have undermined American influence in the Middle East, but would also have endangered the country's standing around the globe.

Hence, from October 14, when the first Military Airlift Command (MAC) aircraft arrived in Israel, to October 24, when the guns fell more or less silent, the United States delivered about 12,000 tons of arms to Israel.[8] In addition to copious amounts of ammunition for tanks, artillery, and aircraft, Israel received arms not previously in its arsenal, such as certain types of air-delivered precision-guided munitions (PGMs). The United States also flew in fighter-bombers to cover the IDF's wartime losses. The combined air- and sealift continued until mid-November, by which time the United States had delivered more than 60,000 tons of arms, eclipsing the total supplied by the Soviet Union to its Arab clients. Only in the category of tanks (and other armored vehicles) did the American arms transfer effort lag behind its Soviet rival.

Arms Transfers and the Golan Front

During the mid-afternoon of October 6, the Syrian and Egyptian armies launched massive simultaneous assaults against IDF positions on the Golan and in the Sinai.[9] To parry these twin thrusts, an unprepared IDF could muster only meager forces. Its reserve formations had not been mobilized and deployed to the fronts prior to the outbreak of fighting, because of a faulty military intelligence assessment about the likelihood of war, combined with poor civilian decision making. On the Golan front, IDF forces were very heavily outnumbered in troops, tanks, and artillery by the attacking Syrian army.

On the northern part of the front, the Syrian army made little progress and suffered grievous losses as the result of an epic mobile defense waged by a single Israeli armored brigade. On the southern part of the front, to the contrary, in spite of suffering similarly grievous losses, the Syrian army made substantial progress in the early hours of the war, penetrating the IDF's defenses in the area and threatening to stream down into Israel proper. Only the speedy arrival of the first IDF reserve formations and Israel Air Force (IAF) efforts, coupled with Syrian hesitation, prevented the southern part of the Golan from falling completely into Arab hands.

CHAPTER 7

Due to the proximity of the Syrian army to the state's northern border, Israel initially gave priority to the Golan front, sending many of the IDF's rapidly mobilizing reserve formations there. By the third day of the war, October 8, enough Israeli reserve forces had entered the battle not only to stabilize the front and stem the Syrian advance, but also to begin pushing the Syrian army back toward the prewar ceasefire line, the so-called Purple Line. By the fifth day of the war, October 10, the IDF had essentially cleared the Israeli-controlled portion of the Golan of Syrian forces.

On the same day, the IDF was authorized to launch a large-scale counteroffensive into Syria, to begin the next day. From October 11–14, the IDF steadily advanced in the direction of the capital of Damascus, breaking through several lines of Syrian army defenses in the process. The IDF halted its offensive once it had acquired enough territory inside Syria for its long-range artillery to threaten the outskirts of Damascus. From this date onward, the sole notable operation initiated by Israeli forces involved the recapture of an intelligence outpost on Mount Hermon that had fallen to the Syrians early in the fighting, as the IDF shifted its attention to the Sinai front. The Syrian army, along with its Iraqi and Jordanian allies, mounted a number of local counterattacks against the Israeli salient inside Syria until the end of the war, but the IDF repulsed these assaults without too much difficulty, inflicting heavy losses on Arab forces.

Early on in the war, Israeli officials complained to their American counterparts that ammunition shortages caused by the delay in sending arms to Israel were hindering IDF operations on the Golan front. These claims, however, appear to have been made primarily in order to place pressure on the United States to set up an arms pipeline, not because Israeli officials genuinely feared that the IDF would be hampered on the Golan in the short run by a lack of munitions.[10] For their part, American officials noted that Israeli forces were indeed conserving certain types of ammunition, but they did not think that the IDF was experiencing any shortages at this stage of the war that could impede its operations.[11] Thus, it is rather doubtful that IDF operations on the Golan front actually suffered as a consequence of insufficient ammunition stockpiles. Whatever the case, it is quite clear that American arms transfers during the Yom Kippur War did not contribute to Israel's victory on the northern front. The IDF had smashed and repelled the Syrian army, and Israel had achieved its major objective on the Golan front, the conquest of additional Syrian territory to be used as a bargaining chip in postwar negotiations, before American arms began to flow to Israel in any appreciable quantities.

Arms Transfers and the Sinai Front

On the Sinai front, the Egyptian army experienced little trouble in crossing the Suez Canal and penetrating 10–20 kilometers into the Sinai, faced as it was by only small numbers of Israeli troops and tanks manning the so-called Bar Lev Line, a rather inflated title for what was in effect nothing more than a string of loosely connected observation posts along the waterline. The Egyptians spent October 6 and 7 consolidating their positions in the Sinai, mopping up the remaining Israeli forces in the area, and preparing for the expected IDF counterattack, which came on October 8. While the Israeli attack failed to throw the Egyptian army back across the Suez Canal and led to substantial losses among two IDF tank battalions, it inflicted considerable casualties on the Egyptian army and essentially stopped the Egyptians from moving further into the Sinai for the moment.

For the next few days, the Sinai front settled down, as each side tentatively probed the other's defensive positions. This situation changed dramatically on October 14, when the Egyptian army attempted a major breakout from its bridgeheads in an effort to seize the vital mountain passes in the Sinai, in part to relieve pressure on the Syrian army then reeling as a result of the IDF counteroffensive into Syria. In one of history's largest tank battles, the IDF destroyed 200–250 Egyptian tanks at very little cost to itself. Israel, which had been waiting for the right opportunity to mount a cross-canal counteroffensive of its own, now deployed the IDF to attack Egypt proper. From October 15 onward, IDF forces crossed the Suez Canal into Egypt, establishing a secure bridgehead, while they simultaneously overran crucial Egyptian positions in the Sinai.

Before a cease-fire agreement more or less went into effect on October 24, the IDF continued to expand its bridgehead on the Egyptian side of the Suez Canal, inflicting very heavy casualties on Egyptian forces in the process. The IDF eventually surrounded one of the two Egyptian corps, the Third Army, which had participated in the initial offensive across the Suez Canal. By the end of the fighting, the IDF had also advanced to within 100 kilometers of the capital, Cairo, and it had occupied more territory in Egypt than the Egyptian army had captured in Sinai.

The impact of American arms transfers on the Sinai front is not as clear-cut as on the Golan front. On the one hand, the tank battle of October 14 and the establishment of an Israeli bridgehead in Egypt on October 15—the turning points in the war on the southern front—occurred just as the American airlift to Israel got underway; therefore,

CHAPTER 7

American arms transfers had no direct effect on these events. One of the Israeli tank division commanders on the southern front later concluded that:

> the IDF [had vanquished] the Egyptian army . . . before reinforcements [of equipment] from the United States reached the front.[12]

And another IDF officer, a tank battalion commander during the war, was equally dismissive of the role of American arms, commenting that:

> In practical terms, not a single U.S. tank arrived in time to take part in the fighting. . . . Air-to-air missiles; a few [fighter-bombers] that, according to the IAF, were superfluous; and a few [antitank weapons] arrived on October 14. The rest of the arms came . . . after the cease-fire.[13]

On the other hand, the knowledge that significant quantities of American arms had begun to arrive in Israel as of October 14 allowed the IDF to expand the scope and intensify the pace of its cross-canal counteroffensive beyond what would otherwise have been feasible. The dean of Israeli military correspondents observed that:

> part of the arriving [American] equipment [was] urgently [sent to] the front. IDF forces [were] expending more ammunition than planners had thought possible. . . . Ammunition [was] . . . now a high priority.[14]

Nevertheless, despite the flow of American arms, the IDF chief of staff complained rather bitterly to fellow general headquarters (GHQ) officers on October 19 that:

> [The airlift] has to be doubled and tripled. . . . The airlift is not working. Ludicrous amounts [of ammunition] arrived today—enough for less than two hours![15]

Though his remarks in this specific instance turned out to be misplaced, as substantial quantities of American-supplied ammunition were at that very moment on their way to IDF forces on the southern front, the chief of staff was correct in his later assessment that the United States exploited the leverage that it gained over Israeli policy through arms transfers to limit the IDF's victory against the Egyptian army.¹⁶ Indeed, American officials compelled Israel to release its grip on the Third Army, thereby reducing the magnitude of the IDF's triumph on the Sinai front, saving Egypt's "honor," and permitting the United States to dominate postwar Arab–Israeli peace negotiations.

On the tactical level of warfare, new American weapons systems, such as the aforementioned air-delivered PGMs, certainly helped the IDF to inflict more destruction on the Egyptian army than would have been the case in their absence, but just as certainly did not cause enough additional damage to affect the outcome of any specific engagement. Air-delivered PGMs, for example, destroyed their targets approximately 80 percent of the time, but only about 80 of them were employed during the war.¹⁷ Moreover, replacement fighter-bombers allowed the air force to play a more active role in the final battles on the Sinai front than would otherwise have been the case. Again, though, this replacement equipment did not fundamentally affect the outcome of any particular engagement.

Summary

Echoing a sentiment widely held by ostensibly informed observers of the Yom Kippur War, a prominent British historian has asserted that, "[Israel] would have almost certainly suffered a crushing defeat but for the rushing of American arms to the front."¹⁸ The historical facts, however, tell a very different story. Overall, American arms transfers made a rather modest contribution to Israel's military victory in the Yom Kippur War. The establishment of the arms pipeline came too late to influence events on the Golan front, as Israel defeated Syria (and its Arab allies) before American assistance began to reach the IDF in significant amounts. On the Sinai front, the tide of battle had turned in favor of Israel before American arms transfers began to reach IDF forces. While these arms bolstered the IDF's cross-canal counteroffensive in the last days of the war, the United States ultimately stepped in to limit Israel's triumph on this front, using arms transfers as leverage to achieve this goal. From a strictly military point of view, then, Israel benefited most from the American arms pipeline after the end of the war, when the IDF rebuilt and expanded its order of battle.

A former head of Israeli military intelligence summed up the impact of the American arms pipeline as follows:

> ... perhaps its major significance was a political one. Its unequivocal nature, as seen by the Soviets and Arabs, who were unaware

of the hesitation and foot-dragging that had taken place . . . for a full and fateful week of fighting, was undoubtedly a major factor in bringing about a cease-fire. . . .[19]

Even though the United States prevented an overwhelming Israeli victory in the Yom Kippur War, in other words, the political symbolism of the airlift helped to ensure that the war came to an end at a point where the IDF clearly held the upper hand on the battlefields. Furthermore, the arms pipeline undoubtedly improved Israel's morale during and after the war, as it demonstrated to Israelis that they were not entirely isolated in a hostile world. And, it surely bears mentioning, the psychological importance of superpower support for a small, beleaguered country with few reliable friends in the international system at a moment of grave national peril should not be dismissed lightly.

Still, the main lesson that Israel drew from the events surrounding the American air- and sealift is that the IDF must be in a position to fight any future war without depending upon resupply from abroad.

8

The American Assessment

The United States displayed a keen interest in the nature, progress, and results of the 1973 Yom Kippur War. Central Intelligence Agency (CIA) analysts and United States Army Training and Doctrine (TRADOC) Command officers thought that, in a number of crucial respects, this war reflected the way in which a nonnuclear military conflict between North Atlantic Treaty Organization (NATO) and Warsaw Pact (WP) military forces would be most likely to unfold on the plains of Central Europe. At the operational (macro) level of warfare, an outnumbered Israel Defense Forces (IDF) had waged a mobile campaign—first on defense, then on offense—of the type envisaged by outnumbered NATO forces. The Egyptian and, especially, Syrian armies, on the other hand, had launched Soviet-inspired offensives in the Sinai and on the Golan, respectively, later resorting to Soviet-inspired defensives in attempts to fend off IDF counteroffensives. The Yom Kippur War, to put it differently, had pitted a Western-style army employing maneuver warfare against Soviet-style armies relying first and foremost on attrition warfare. At the tactical (micro) level of warfare, some of the most advanced Western arms had faced off against some of the most advanced Soviet arms. State-of-the-art American aircraft in the Israeli arsenal had confronted state-of-the-art Soviet antiaircraft systems in Arab arsenals. Likewise, modern American and British tanks in the Israeli arsenal had confronted modern Soviet antitank missiles and rockets in Arab arsenals.

Militarily speaking, Israel won the Yom Kippur War, so the IDF found itself largely in control of the postwar battlefields. American intelligence analysts and military officers, therefore, had ample opportunities to visit the Golan and Sinai battlefields to assess firsthand the nature, progress, and results of the fighting.[1] They also had ready access to counterparts in Israel who shared their knowledge and expe-

CHAPTER 8

riences of the recent war.² One senior TRADOC officer at the time of the war related that:

> We talked to most of the battalion and brigade and all of the division commanders who had fought. We went to the Golan ... and to the Sinai. We walked on the ground where the battles had been fought, usually with the guys who had fought them.³

Speaking about a group of senior IDF armored corps officers, and echoing the sentiments of his American colleagues, he also commented that, "We learned an enormous amount from all of them, and we really owe them a great debt. With their experience and background ... they identified things about which we were unsure."⁴

These visits and talks gave birth to numerous classified intelligence and military reports on various aspects of the war, some of them quite massive, multivolume tomes filled with all manner of technical data. Much of these data remain locked away in government archives, making it difficult to know with complete certainty how American intelligence analysts and military officers viewed the Yom Kippur War. But sufficient information has now come to light to draw a reasonably well-rounded picture of how they understood the war.

This claim, of course, requires some elaboration. In the summer of 2012, the CIA declassified a report titled *The 1973 Arab–Israeli War: Overview and Analysis of the Conflict* (hereafter simply referred to as the "CIA report" or "the report").⁵ This document, a 125-page survey of the war that was circulated to select high-ranking American officials in September 1975, and which relies heavily on still-classified intelligence and military reports for its data and conclusions, is remarkably intact in its declassified version.⁶ Insofar as concerns the substantive portions of the report, the only lines of text struck from the declassified version are those that identify particular confidential sources of information, whether American or Israeli.⁷

The CIA report's findings can be considered as broadly indicative of the official American understanding of the Yom Kippur War for two reasons. First, the report draws heavily on an extensive range of other intelligence and military reports. And, second, its data and conclusions dovetail nicely with the views expressed by prominent military officers who evaluated the war for the Defense Department. The CIA report, consequently, is the single most valuable source presently available for elucidating the specifics of the official American perspective on the war, some curious omissions and minor inaccuracies notwithstanding. It is now possible, in other words, not only to speak about the lessons that intelligence analysts and military officers derived from the war with greater authority than before, but also to open a window into their take on the nature, progress, and results of the fighting itself.

The CIA report is organized around four central themes: the war in the air, the war on the Golan front, the war on the Sinai front, and the basic lessons of the war. This framework seems as good as any in laying out the official American interpretation of the nature, progress, and results of the Yom Kippur War.

The War in the Air

The duel between the Israel Air Force (IAF), on the one hand, and the Egyptian and Syrian integrated air defense systems (IADSs), on the other hand, intensely interested the United States, particularly in light of the WP's reliance on the same air defense weapons and doctrine to thwart NATO airpower. In contrast to the claim of many observers of the Yom Kippur War, who leaped to the conclusion—on the basis of the IAF's unprecedented (for it) losses in the fighting—that IADSs would severely reduce the effectiveness of airpower on future battlefields, the CIA report adopts a more cautious and nuanced view of the encounter between Israeli airpower and Arab air defenses.

It observes that, in terms of destroying IAF aircraft, Arab air defenses were not especially potent, managing to shoot down about 80 fighter-bombers, approximately 55 percent falling to surface-to-air missile (SAM) batteries and approximately 45 percent falling to anti-aircraft artillery (AAA) batteries, either operating alone or in tandem with SAM batteries.[8] The overall IAF loss rate to Arab IADSs—calculated by dividing the total number of aircraft lost to SAM and AAA batteries by the total number of sorties flown in the face of these batteries—was no higher—and may possibly have been even lower—in the Yom Kippur War than in the 1967 Six-Day War, when Egypt and Syria possessed far less comprehensive and sophisticated air defense capabilities.[9]

The report also observes that Syria's IADS proved to be considerably more effective than Egypt's, inflicting losses on the IAF at a rate three times greater than its Egyptian counterpart.[10] The reason for its superior efficiency, according to the CIA report, stemmed not from the superior professionalism of its operators, but rather from circumstances related to the geography of the battlefields. The Golan front was much closer to Israel proper than the Sinai front, so the IAF was called upon to support hard-pressed and heavily outnumbered ground

CHAPTER 8

forces in the north to a greater extent than in the south—where it exercised considerable prudence after its initial exposure to the Egyptian IADS—in order to prevent a Syrian breakthrough into Israeli territory.[11]

The most important effect of Arab IADSs on the battlefields, notes the CIA report, lay in reducing the impact of IAF close air support (CAS) and interdiction strikes on the Egyptian and Syrian armies throughout much of the war. The report states that:

> The Arabs had weapons designed to provide overlapping coverage to [high] altitudes. . . . This meant that there was no airspace over the battlefield within which the IAF could operate free of threat. The electronic systems associated with these weapons operated in many different bands of the radio spectrum. This meant that no fighter could carry enough gear for electronic countermeasures (ECM) to defend itself against all threats. Moreover, the Israelis had no ECM gear to cope with some Arab systems. . . . Thus, despite the fact that the IAF had learned how to cope with some air defense weapons rather well . . . [it] had to recognize that the sheer size and variety of weapons it would face over Arab[-held] territory would greatly hinder the accomplishment of its ground support mission and threaten high losses.[12]

It also remarks that:

> The Israelis found that if they stayed [at medium altitude,] they could cope with [Arab] air defense weapons. At [medium altitude,] they were above the effective range of AAA, their ECM and tactics against [some types of SAM] were effective enough to make the risks of operating at [these altitudes] acceptable, and their pilots had sufficient warning of [the] launch [of a more advanced type of SAM] to take evasive action. However, the combination of altitude and evasive maneuvering severely degraded the accuracy of IAF weapons delivery.[13]

The IAF often resorted to "loft" attacks, in which bombs were rather ineffectively "tossed" in the general directions of their targets.[14]

The IAF did at times ably assist IDF ground forces by flying into the teeth of Arab IADSs, as it did on the Golan front during the early days of the war, when its interdiction strikes mauled Syrian army supply columns, thereby helping to contain the Syrian offensive;

however, the IAF did so at substantial cost to itself. Only toward the end of the war and only on the Sinai front, after IDF ground forces had crossed to the Egyptian side of the Suez Canal, smashing much of the Egyptian IADS in the process, did the IAF engage in effective CAS and interdiction strikes at limited cost to itself. Throughout much of the war, the IAF played a rather marginal role on the battlefields in order to conserve its aircraft and prevent unacceptable losses, a development that aided the Arab war effort.

Whether the IAF could have mounted a more robust and effectual air campaign in support of IDF ground forces had it been able to engage in sustained attacks against the Arab IADSs at the outset of hostilities, as envisaged in its prewar operational plans, is not speculated upon by the CIA analysts, who perhaps sought to stick to the facts of the war rather than to engross themselves in "counterfactual" analysis. Still, in light of the crucial importance NATO attributed to the defeat of WP air defenses, omitting any mention of the manner in which the IAF intended to tackle Arab IADSs versus the manner in which it actually tackled them constitutes a significant oversight.

In the years prior to the Yom Kippur War, the IAF developed intricate operational plans to knock out Arab IADSs at the outset of the next war. The IAF preferred to implement Model 5 and Challenge 4, the code names of the final iterations of the plans to destroy the Syrian and Egyptian IADSs, respectively, in the form of a preemptive strike. Though Israel had only a few hours of early warning of the Syrian and Egyptian offensives, the IAF nevertheless had enough time to at least begin to implement these plans before the Arab offensives got underway. Under intense American pressure, however, the Israeli government refused to sanction a preemptive strike.[15]

Many informed analysts believe that an IAF preemptive strike would have completely changed the complexion of the war. Emblematic of this perspective, two analysts later calculated that the IAF could have knocked out 90 percent of the Syrian and Egyptian SAM batteries "in a period of three to six hours for the loss of under [10] aircraft." With air superiority over the Golan and Sinai essentially assured as a result, according to this line of thinking, IAF intervention in the ground war would have been swift and massive, its fighter-bombers dropping "[3,000] tons of bombs on enemy targets before the Arab attack reached full strength."[16]

The refusal to authorize a preemptive strike, coupled with the desperate straits in which IDF ground forces on the Golan and in the Sinai found themselves at the outbreak of the war, meant that the IAF could not concentrate its full attention on Arab IADSs at the outset of hostilities. Rather, it had to attack these air defenses while simultaneously coming to the assistance of these forces, a scenario that it had not taken seriously before the war. A hastily improvised attempt to carry out operation Model 5 on the second day of the war failed to put a dent in the Syrian IADS, while an initially successful attempt to execute Challenge 4 earlier that day was canceled by IDF general headquarters (GHQ) in order to divert the IAF to the north to help fend off a potential Syrian breakthrough on the Golan.[17] Consequently, the IAF never overcame the Syrian IADS and only punched holes in the Egyptian IADS during the last week of the war, in a joint effort with ground forces, seriously impeding its ability to support those forces throughout much of the war. None of this information or argumentation made it into the CIA's report, though its authors were well aware that Israel had contemplated a preemptive strike.

The report deals in a more perfunctory manner with Israeli air defences.[18] It points out that, to counter the Egyptian and Syrian air forces, the IAF relied primarily on air-to-air combat, in which its aircraft reigned supreme. The report credits IAF aircraft with 334 victories as against six losses, for a 56:1 "kill ratio."[19] Based on more recent and accurate information, these numbers overestimate the number of IAF victories and underestimate the number of its losses.[20] Nevertheless, it is unquestionably the case that the IAF dominated the skies in air-to-air combat throughout the war, preventing the Egyptian and Syrian air forces, with rare exceptions, from executing effective CAS and interdiction strikes against Israeli targets. Israel also possessed an IADS of its own, which performed well during the war. The CIA report credits it with the destruction of 100 Arab aircraft—22 by SAM batteries and 78 by AAA batteries.[21] Again, though these figures, particularly the number of AAA victories, are exaggerated (the genuine number of Arab aircraft downed by Israeli ground-based air defenses is closer to 50), it would appear that the Israeli IADS actually outperformed those of its Arab counterparts, despite its considerably smaller proportions.

Another airpower-related topic oddly overlooked by the CIA report, but of significant interest to the American military establishment, involved the performance of American precision-guided munitions (PGMs) during the war, especially new types supplied to the IAF in the final days of hostilities. Though used in small numbers—and though not affecting the results of any ground battles—these PGMs achieved a hit rate of 75–85 per cent.[22] The military establishment considered PGMs to be the wave of the future, so it took heart from their performance in the Yom Kippur War.

The War on the Golan Front

The Yom Kippur War opened with simultaneous Egyptian and Syrian assaults in the mid-afternoon of October 6. Due to a combination of faulty intelligence analysis and poor governmental decision making, the bulk of the IDF's ground forces were not mobilized and deployed to the fronts prior to the commencement of hostilities. Consequently, the IDF had to absorb the first blow in the face of overwhelming Syrian superiority in men and machines. The Syrians had a roughly 5:1 advantage in tanks, a 10:1 advantage in infantry, and a 12–13:1 advantage in artillery tubes at the outset of the fighting.[23] To counter this numerical disadvantage in tanks, infantry, and artillery tubes, the CIA report comments, the IDF resorted to a mobile defense, constantly moving its tank and artillery forces to meet the most menacing Syrian advances.[24]

On the northern Golan, a lone Israeli tank brigade, with minor reinforcements from other units, fought an epic "blocking battle," which not only prevented the Syrian army from making any real headway in this sector, but also cost the latter hundreds of destroyed tanks (as well as hundreds of other destroyed armored vehicles) in just a few days of fighting.[25] The Israeli defenders repelled wave after wave of Syrian tanks by relying on their outstanding marksmanship and by exploiting the rocky terrain to conceal themselves.

On the southern Golan, in contrast, the Syrian army—faced by more thinly spread IDF forces—initially made some headway in penetrating Israeli defenses, overrunning chunks of territory lost in the Six-Day War. The report mentions:

> ... [that] the scattering of [Israeli] tanks may have saved both the [IDF forces in the area] and the Israeli hold on the [southern] Golan. If the [IDF forces in the area] had been deployed as a compact unit[, they] might have been overrun or shattered by the initial Syrian rush. As it happened, small groups of Israeli tanks maintained their organization and conducted a series of holding actions, each of which by constant resistance sapped the strength of the Syrian forces....[26]

These small-unit actions, in other words, helped to buy sufficient time for the lead elements of the IDF's reserve forces to ascend the southern Golan, join the fighting, and stabilize the front in this sector.

Though the CIA report astutely observes that Israeli small-unit leadership was one of the keys to the IDF's successful defensive stand on the Golan, it does not reflect upon how the relationships among IDF

CHAPTER 8

GHQ, northern front headquarters (HQ), and division commanders and their subordinates affected the fighting. In contrast to the Sinai front, where IDF ground forces experienced all sorts of command and control (C^2) problems during the opening days of the war, C^2 of forces on the Golan was exemplary, another key to the IDF's victory here.[27] Why the report did not assess the IDF's performance on the Golan versus its performance in the Sinai in this respect is unclear. Regardless of the reason, this omission constitutes another significant oversight on the part of the CIA analysts. One would think, after all, that C^2 issues were of immediate relevance to a potential NATO–WP military confrontation.

Despite an overwhelming numerical advantage, the Syrian army's assault essentially petered out after less than two days of fighting.[28] By the third day of the war, October 8, enough Israeli reserve units had reached the front for the IDF to begin a counterattack to clear the Israeli-held part of the Golan. One senior TRADOC officer believed that the IDF's decision to concentrate its reserve units for a counteroffensive rather than parcel them out piecemeal for defense demonstrated that boldness and aggressiveness count for much more on the battlefield than sheer numbers.[29] Whatever the case, by the end of the fifth day of the war, October 10, the IDF had repulsed the Syrian army from the area, with the exception of an intelligence-gathering facility on the slopes of Mount Hermon, which Israel would retake in the final days of the war. The IDF's superiority in maneuver warfare once again proved to be a "game winner."

On October 11, the IDF launched a counteroffensive into Syria, with the aim of capturing additional territory that could be used as a postwar bargaining chip. The CIA report correctly mentions that the Israeli advance was rather cautious, with the IDF moving "in a manner designed to minimize casualties by using heavy tank and artillery fire to open the way [instead of] making costly armor charges."[30] By this point in the war, the IDF sought to conserve its forces for its planned counteroffensive in the Sinai. The northern counteroffensive came to a halt on October 14, when the IDF had advanced to within artillery range of the Syrian capital, Damascus. Indeed, the IDF subjected several targets in the Damascus suburbs to occasional bombardment to drive home the notion that the Syrian capital was not beyond Israel's reach.

From October 15 to October 24, when a stable cease-fire went into effect, Israel was mainly content to hold its positions on the Golan front, shifting the focus of its war effort to the Sinai front. The Syrian army, along with Iraqi and Jordanian expeditionary forces, attempted to mount several local counterattacks against the Israeli enclave inside Syria from October 16 onward, but the IDF repelled these attacks without too much difficulty. In so doing, the IDF was aided on at least one occasion by the faulty coordination among Syrian, Iraqi, and Jordanian forces, which saw the Syrian army heavily bombard its allies, resulting in what the CIA report labeled a "tragic fiasco."[31]

The War on the Sinai Front

IDF forces on the Sinai front were even more heavily outnumbered than they were on the Golan front at the outset of hostilities. Israeli forces consisted of fewer than 500 infantrymen manning a string of fortifications along the Suez Canal, collectively—and grandiosely—known as the Bar Lev Line. This line, as the CIA report remarks, "was not intended to be a desert Maginot Line. . . . The Israeli defensive concepts [sic] did not envisage stopping the Egyptians at the canal's edge."[32] Rather, the line constituted a series of forward strongpoints whose purpose was to report on Egyptian activity along the canal and to harass any Egyptian forces that might cross to the Israeli side of the waterway. A few score tanks, some scattered in small groups, backed up the strongpoints, as did a comparative handful of artillery tubes. Facing this small force, the Egyptians mustered two army corps—the Second and Third—that had at their disposal more than 1,000 tanks and at least 2,000 artillery tubes.[33]

In light of the gross imbalance of forces along the canal, the five divisions involved in the initial Egyptian assault had little trouble crossing to the Israeli side all along the canal, capturing many of the Bar Lev Line strongpoints, and penetrating 10–20 kilometers inland, where they quickly fortified their bridgeheads. The Israeli response to this assault consisted primarily of unsupported "tank charges" by small units in ultimately futile efforts to relieve besieged Bar Lev Line positions. The IDF lost over 150 tanks—approximately 175 if mechanical breakdowns are taken into account—during the first day of the war, many to Egyptian infantrymen armed with antitank missiles and rockets.[34]

Nevertheless—and once more in contrast to many observers of the Yom Kippur War, who leaped to the conclusion that the tank would no longer be dominant on the future battlefield as a result of the impact of antitank missiles and rockets—the CIA report takes a more cautious and nuanced view of the effectiveness of antitank weapons in the war. It cogently states that:

> In the first two or three days of the war, the Egyptian antitank system[s] inflicted heavy losses on the Israelis when they tried to use their armor according to the 1967 pattern [i.e., unsupported by infantry and artillery]. The most effective use of the antitank [systems] was made from fixed defensive positions. Subsequently, however, the Israelis learned to spot potential ambush sites, recognized . . . firing signatures and likely launch points, and began operating in conjunction with infantry teams to defeat the antitank [systems]. By the end of the 1973 war, the Israelis' armored forces had learned to operate effectively[,] despite Egypt's antitank [systems].[35]

The report also notes that antitank weapons were essentially ineffective on the Golan, because the hilly and rocky terrain there made them difficult to deploy.[36] A postwar survey of destroyed Israeli tanks carried out by American military officers reached the conclusion that no more than 25 percent of IDF losses—and quite possibly a much smaller percentage—could be attributed to antitank missiles and rockets.[37] The tank remained the king of the battlefield during the Yom Kippur War.

The CIA report ascribes these heavy IDF tank losses at the beginning of hostilities to faulty tactics. The report is right to do so. The lack of infantry and artillery support during the first days of the war certainly rendered Israeli tanks very vulnerable when they attacked into the teeth of Egyptian defenses; faulty tactics alone, however, are not enough to account for the IDF losses. The IDF's poor C^2 in the Sinai proved equally responsible for these losses.[38] Bickering and confusion among IDF GHQ, southern command HQ, and division commanders and their subordinates resulted in poor decision making (e.g., in not authorizing a rapid withdrawal of endangered Bar Lev Line strongpoints) and disorganized, piecemeal relief efforts by isolated tank forces acting largely on their own.

These same C^2 problems were in evidence when the IDF launched a major counterattack on Egyptian positions on October 8, after two reserve tank divisions had arrived in Sinai.[39] The attack initially made some progress, but quickly bogged down, as unsupported IDF tank forces once more suffered substantial losses at the hands of Egyptian antitank missiles and rockets. The CIA report makes no mention of the crippling effect of C^2 problems on the Israeli attack—C^2 problems that kept one of the two tank divisions moving around in circles throughout the battle, while the other division engaged in uncoordinated thrusts toward Egyptian positions.[40]

Despite its defeat, the Israeli counterattack, whose purpose was to roll up Egyptian defensive positions from north to south and, perhaps, to seize one of the Egyptian army's bridges across the canal, essentially checked any further Egyptian advances for the moment. From October 9–13, both the IDF and the Egyptian army were largely content to hold their positions, occasionally probing the other side's defenses, in what the CIA report jokingly referred to as a "sitzkrieg."[41]

On October 14, the Egyptian army—in part in an attempt to relieve pressure on the Syrian army on the Golan and in part in an attempt to reach the Sinai mountain passes as dictated by phase two of its Soviet-inspired operational plan—launched a major offensive into the teeth of three IDF tank divisions.[42] Masters of the kind of mobile warfare necessitated by this offensive, the Israelis had no trouble defeating every Egyptian army thrust, destroying 200–250 Egyptian tanks at little cost to themselves and setting the stage for the IDF to launch a cross-canal offensive of its own.

From October 15, when the first IDF forces crossed over into "Africa" (i.e., the Egyptian side of the Suez Canal), until October 24, when a more or less stable cease-fire came into effect, the Israelis were on the offensive, the Egyptians on the defensive.[43] The IDF simultaneously attacked Egyptian positions on both sides of the canal, as well as repelled Egyptian efforts to choke off the Israeli bridgehead. One senior TRADOC officer, undoubtedly employing a touch of hyperbole, described the fighting during this stage of the war as follows:

> When the cross-Suez battlefield became fluid, the IDF . . . destroyed 90 percent of the defending Egyptian tanks with no IDF losses, sweeping up the canal banks, destroying Egyptian [antitank missile] positions where crews had been destroyed or driven from their positions by suppressive fires [sic] of artillery or by infantry.[44]

On the Egyptian side of the canal, IDF forces quickly fanned out, overrunning SAM and AAA batteries, opening up undefended flight corridors, which in turn allowed the IAF to engage in effective CAS and interdiction strikes on behalf of ground forces. By the end of the war, the IDF had advanced to within 100 kilometers of the Egyptian capital, Cairo, held more territory on the Egyptian side of the canal than Egypt held on the Israeli side, and had surrounded the Egyptian Third Army corps (though American diplomatic intervention ultimately compelled the IDF to release its grip on the Egyptians).

CHAPTER 8

Basic Lessons of the War

American intelligence analysts and military officers drew a number of fundamental conclusions from the Yom Kippur War.[45] First, the results of the fighting, particularly on the Golan front, bolstered the validity of NATO's contemporary operational plan, which was based upon a frontier defense of Central Europe. To counter a WP invasion, in other words, NATO envisaged waging a mobile campaign at the West German border, relying on the qualitative superiority of its forces to stop their more numerous foe in its tracks, only then moving over to a counteroffensive of its own. American intelligence analysts and military officers took heart from the fact that:

> ... the tenacity and adaptability of small units and their immediate leaders enabled the Israelis to stabilize the front and go over to the offensive so quickly. This was especially evident on the Golan, where Israeli forces, though [heavily] outnumbered ... in almost every category of equipment, were able to stop the Syrian advance within 24 hours and eliminate it within 72 hours.[46]

In the Yom Kippur War, the IDF had shown that a Western-oriented army—with the proper training, leadership, and tactics—could not only quickly recover from an invasion by Soviet-oriented, numerically superior armies, but could also defeat them in rather short order without sacrificing large tracts of territory in the process.

Second, the results of the fighting reinforced in the minds of American intelligence analysts and military officers the importance of "combined arms"—the idea that, for an army to prevail on the battlefield, all of its different components (e.g., its intelligence, tank, infantry, artillery, engineer, and air forces) must work together in a seamless web to overcome a foe. The CIA report sensibly remarks that "the battlefield ... is a complicated environment and no one weapon or arm of service can function effectively on it without the active aid and cooperation of others."[47] One senior TRADOC officer commented similarly that "the density–intensity–lethality equation will prevent [future] domination of the battle by any single weapons system; to win, it will be necessary to employ all battlefield systems in closely coordinated all-arms actions."[48] And the head of TRADOC at the time of the Yom Kippur War commented that, "The Israelis demonstrated [that] it is possible to operate successfully in the face of highly lethal weapons by effective use of the combined arms team[:] that is[,] tanks supported by mechanized infantry, self-propelled artillery, and self-propelled air defense weapons."⁴⁹

American intelligence analysts and military officers presciently retained their faith in the efficacy of both tanks and aircraft. The CIA report observes that:

> The effectiveness of [Soviet antitank missiles and rockets] was described in almost mythical proportions in the immediate aftermath of the 1973 war. The evidence now available supports a much more realistic appraisal. Antitank weapons... took a heavy toll of Israeli armor. But they did not render the tank obsolete. The initial impression created by the Egyptian use of [antitank weapons] was artificially reinforced by the inappropriate tactics used by the Israelis in the first few days of the war.⁵⁰

The most destructive antitank weapon on the battlefield remained the tank. At least 90 percent of Arab tanks destroyed in the Yom Kippur War and at least 75 percent of Israeli tanks destroyed in the war were knocked out by other tanks.⁵¹ As for aircraft, while they might no longer be able to operate with as much freedom over the battlefield as in the past, they could still deliver highly effective CAS and interdiction strikes (especially with PGMs, as demonstrated by the IAF's employment of these weapons in the last days of the fighting), so long as the opponent's IADS had been dealt with beforehand through a combined arms effort.

Third, the sheer deadliness of the modern battlefield surprised intelligence analysts and military officers. The head of TRADOC asserted "that modern weapons are vastly more lethal than any weapons we have encountered on the battlefield before."⁵² He went on to point out that, "Egypt and Syria lost approximately 1,500 to 2,000 tanks. That would equate to all the tanks we have in Europe. [They lost] five hundred artillery tubes...; [this number] is almost equal [to] the [total] amount of artillery [we have] in Europe."⁵³ And he added that, "if the rate of loss which occurred in the ... war during the short period of 18 to 20 days were extrapolated to the battlefields of Europe over a period of 60 to 90 days, the resulting losses would reach levels for which the United States Army is not prepared in any way."⁵⁴ Another senior TRADOC officer noted that combined Israeli and Arab tank losses in just the first week of the Yom Kippur War exceeded the total number of tanks that the United States Army had in Europe at the time.⁵⁵

The way to avoid these potential losses in a future war, determined American intelligence analysts and military officers, was to enhance

CHAPTER 8

the training and tactics of the American army. "[I]t is essential," wrote the head of TRADOC, "[that] we have a highly trained and highly skilled combined arms team of armor, infantry, artillery, and air defense backed up by the support required to sustain combat operations." He went on to say that, "[T]he training of the individual as well as the team will make the difference between success and failure on the battlefield. Well trained Israeli[s] . . . made the difference in 1973."[56] Another senior TRADOC officer expressed himself even more emphatically on this theme when he said of the lessons of the Yom Kippur War that:

> In modern battle, regardless of which side outnumbers the other, and regardless of who attacks whom, the outcome of battle at the tactical and operational levels will be decided by factors other than numbers and other than who attacks and who defends. In the end[,] the side that somehow, at some time, somewhere in the course of battle seizes the initiative and holds it to the end will be the side that wins. More often than not[,] the outcome of battle defies the traditional calculus used to predict such outcomes. It is strikingly evident that battles are yet won by the courage of soldiers, the character of leaders, and the combat excellence of well-trained units—beginning with crews, platoons, companies, battalions, and squadrons and ending with regiments, brigades, divisions, and corps. The best tank on the battlefield is yet the one with the best crew. The best units on the battlefield are those that are well trained and well led[,] and those who have trained together to a high level of excellence before the battle's onset.[57]

American intelligence analysts and military officers, of course, drew many other conclusions from the results of the Yom Kippur War, on issues ranging from age-old supply and logistics concerns to the latest developments in electronic warfare in the air, at sea, and on land. Nevertheless, the belief that the higher-quality few could defeat the lower-quality many, the belief that a combined arms approach to fighting would be essential in the future, and the belief that modern weapons would cause unprecedented loss rates on the battlefield were certainly among the most important findings to come out of an analysis of the war.

THE AMERICAN ASSESSMENT

Summary

An official who read the CIA's description and analysis of the Yom Kippur War scribbled "very interesting report" on its front cover. Indeed, not only is the report fascinating in and of itself, but it also exemplifies the sober, measured perspective adopted by American intelligence analysts and military officers with respect to the nature, progress, and results of the war, its omissions and inaccuracies notwithstanding. Unlike many observers of the fighting, who claimed that the Yom Kippur War represented a revolution in warfare, at least in the sense that advanced antiaircraft and antitank weapons had rendered the aircraft and the tank largely impotent (if not entirely obsolete) on the modern battlefield, American intelligence analysts and military officers wisely concluded that no such revolution had taken place. Rather, they insightfully asserted that heavy IDF losses in aircraft and tanks in the opening days of the war were not so much a consequence of advanced technologies, but instead were caused primarily by the lopsided force ratios faced by the IDF on both the Golan and Sinai fronts at the outset of the war in tandem with faulty Israeli tactics, especially in regard to unsupported "tank charges." (They should also have added C^2 problems to the mix on the Sinai front.) Once the IDF recovered from its initial shock, deployed its reserves, and improvised new tactics, they noted, its aircraft and tanks not only suffered far fewer losses, but they also spearheaded the Israeli victory in the war.

The results of the Yom Kippur War served to reinforce in the mindset of American intelligence analysts and military officers some long-standing and tried-and-true basics about warfare, particularly that the superior few could defeat the inferior many, given the appropriate training and leadership, and that a combined arms approach at the operational and tactical levels of fighting offered the best prospect of victory on the battlefield at a tolerable cost in men and machines. For them, in short, the Yom Kippur War represented not a revolution but rather an evolution in the nature of war.

9

The Israeli Response

For the Israeli defense establishment, as for the Israeli populace, the 1973 Yom Kippur War constituted a profoundly unsettling experience. Beyond the initial shock caused by the Egyptian and Syrian surprise attack, and beyond the enduring pain over the heavy personnel losses suffered by the Israel Defense Forces (IDF) during the ensuing three-week war, the defense establishment could not but acknowledge the disturbing reality that some of the most strongly held assumptions underlying Israel's defense posture in the years prior to the Yom Kippur War had turned out to be thoroughly misguided when push came to shove.

The Agranat Commission—an investigative body composed of prominent retired jurists and generals whose mandate included probing the IDF's mistaken intelligence assessment on the eve of the war, its unpreparedness for battle, and the consequent battlefield setbacks at the outbreak of the war, especially on the Sinai front—offered perhaps the first in-depth critique of Israel's defense posture before the war. Released in its final form in January 1975, the commission's report highlighted fundamental flaws in the IDF's processing of intelligence data and in its combat readiness on the eve of the war, as well as serious command and control (C^2) problems during the early days of hostilities, again particularly on the southern front, and urged a series of reforms to avoid a repeat of these mistakes.[1]

Based on the recommendations of the Agranat Commission report, as well as on the lessons learned by the IDF itself as a result of its experience in the war, the Israeli defense establishment took a close look at the IDF's force structure and war-fighting doctrine in the years after 1973. While reaffirming its faith in certain elements of the IDF's force structure and war-fighting doctrine, the defense establishment also initiated numerous reforms in an effort to prevent a repeat of the mistakes made prior to the Yom Kippur War. Simultaneously, the defense establishment also grappled with the reorganization of Israel's intelligence community.

Intelligence Reforms

The Agranat Commission members, like all other informed observers of the war, concluded that IDF military intelligence, A'MAN, bore much of the responsibility for Israel's setbacks in the early days of hostilities. The problem lay not with its collection of intelligence data, but rather with its analysis of that information.[2] A'MAN, after all, had nearly complete and highly accurate data on the Egyptian and Syrian armies' capabilities: their orders of battle, the disposition of their forces, their plans of attack, the quantity and quality of their weapons, and so forth. And, several days prior to the outbreak of hostilities, A'MAN had informed both IDF general headquarters (GHQ) and the civilian government that the Egyptian and Syrian armies massed along the borders were now in a position to initiate a war with Israel at any moment. Rather, the problem lay in the realm of intelligence analysis. Despite issuing a "war warning," A'MAN continued to insist that Egypt and Syria had no intention of going to war with Israel—that hostilities remained a low probability event—an estimate upon which IDF GHQ and the civilian government relied in making decisions about how to handle the threatening situation on the state's borders. A'MAN only reversed this estimate a few hours before hostilities broke out; by then, however, the IDF could not be mobilized and deployed to meet the Egyptian and Syrian attacks in strength.

Many informed observers would later chalk up Israel's intelligence fiasco to hubris, a feeling of overwhelming self-confidence that was said to be pervasive not only throughout A'MAN and the IDF, but also throughout Israeli society in general, in the aftermath of the 1967 Six-Day War. One eminent historian, based on his personal observations, summed up the problem succinctly this way:

> But what was most injurious [about the outcome of the Six-Day War] was the effect it had on the Israelis' mind-set [sic], from top to bottom.... The disease of hubris infected the nation from top to bottom.[3]

This hubris, according to these observers, bred a certain amount of contempt for the capabilities of Israel's Arab foes, a contempt that fed directly into the state's undeniable complacency on the eve of the Yom Kippur War.

Regardless of the deeper explanation for Israel's unpreparedness for war, aside from calling for the immediate dismissal of the officers deemed most culpable for this fiasco—namely A'MAN's commanding officer, his deputy, and a couple of mid-level officers attached to the IDF's southern command—the Agranat Commission made a number of recommendations for reform in the intelligence sphere that were accepted by the IDF and the civilian government. Within A'MAN itself, analysis from this point forward would focus more intently on a potential opponent's capabilities to wage war against Israel than on its intentions to do so. Moreover, a "devil's advocate" unit was created to inhibit the tendency toward "groupthink," a psychological tendency in which dissenting voices within an organization are eventually brought around to the majority's way of thinking through subtle peer pressure. This unit would serve as a "reality check" on the prevailing strain of thinking within A'MAN by offering an alternative analysis of the intelligence data at hand. Outside of A'MAN, the Agranat Commission urged the creation of a national security council (NSC) to advise the prime minister, as well as the strengthening of the foreign ministry's research and analysis unit, both in order to dilute AMAN's traditional dominance over national intelligence estimates. A former IDF chief of staff who took command of the Sinai front during the Yom Kippur War summed up the reasoning for the creation of independent analytical voices when he said that "the processing of intelligence estimates through a number of independent agencies can prevent . . . misconceptions."[4]

Israel has not suffered an intelligence fiasco similar to the one it sustained on the eve of the Yom Kippur War in the decades since 1973. Nevertheless, determining the extent to which reforms in the intelligence community are responsible for sparing Israel from a repeat of this kind of fiasco is not at all easy. The reforms notwithstanding, critics claim, not much has really changed in the intelligence community over the years since the Yom Kippur War. A'MAN remains the central voice in respect of providing national intelligence estimates to the IDF and the civilian government. Neither the NSC nor the foreign ministry has enjoyed much influence over this endeavor. Indeed, a strong case can be made that regional developments in the Middle East over the past few decades rather than procedural improvements inside the intelligence community should be credited for the fact that Israel has not been subjected to another crushing strategic surprise since 1973. The 1979 Egyptian–Israeli and 1994 Jordanian–Israeli peace treaties, after all, significantly reduced the capability of the Arab world to engage in a full-scale war against Israel, a trend that has been substantially reinforced over the past two decades by the virtual disintegration of such key Middle Eastern states as Iraq and, later, Syria.

Force Structure Reforms

Vladimir Lenin is reputed to be the source of the quip that "quantity has a quality all its own." Regardless of whether he is the father of this remark, the idea that underlies it contains more than a little merit insofar as concerns the battlefield. Numbers in themselves might not be a decisive element in warfare, but they can go a long way toward offsetting any advantages possessed by a less numerous but qualitatively superior opponent. Numbers, in short, count. Prior to the Yom Kippur War, the Israeli defense establishment had always steadfastly adhered to the principle that the "few" could overcome the "many" if the few were sufficiently superior to the many in quality. After the war, the Israeli defense establishment continued to adhere to this principle; however, it also decided to hedge its bet by drastically expanding the IDF's order of battle.

A few statistics will suffice to illustrate that the Israeli defense establishment clearly absorbed the lesson about the effectiveness of numbers on the battlefield. The standing forces, composed of a mixture of professional soldiers and conscripts, increased from about 75,000 men (and women) prior to 1973 to about 170,000 in the decade following the war, an increase of 130 percent. Similarly, the reserves ballooned from approximately 275,000 men (and women) before the Yom Kippur War to approximately 450,000 in the decade following the war. The number of tanks in the IDF's inventory doubled in the 10 years after the war, while the number of armored personnel carriers (APCs) increased fourfold. Furthermore, the IDF's stock of "consumables"— that is, munitions, spare parts, POL (petroleum, oil, and lubricants), and so on—doubled in the years after the war, increasing from about a two-week supply to about a four-week supply.[5] The defense establishment's decision to stock up on consumables stemmed from its desire to ensure that the IDF could fight the next war to its conclusion without relying on supplies from abroad, a decision taken in response to the delayed American air- and sealift to Israel during the Yom Kippur War, which meant that American arms shipments during the hostilities had only a very limited impact on the IDF's fortunes on the battlefield.

Lest it be thought that the Israeli defense establishment focused solely on quantity in its force structure reforms, the quality of the IDF's acquisitions in the post-1973 years was equally impressive. The Israel

Air Force (IAF) not only received the most advanced American fighter-bombers, but also highly sophisticated electronic countermeasures (ECM) equipment and precision-guided munitions (PGMs) from both American and Israeli industry, not to mention unmanned aerial vehicles (UAVs), a field in which Israel quickly became a world leader. The ground forces received advanced Israeli-designed and Israeli-constructed tanks, the latest American armored personnel carriers (APCs), self-propelled artillery tubes, and engineering vehicles, as well as all kinds of modern American and Israeli infantry weapons, particularly antitank missiles. And the Israel Navy (IN) expanded its inventory of sophisticated fast patrol boats (FPBs) equipped with antiship missiles.

Like its American counterpart, the Israeli defense establishment did not endorse the conclusion that the arrival of sophisticated antitank and air defense weapons signaled the demise of the tank and the aircraft. Rather, like its American counterpart, the defense establishment maintained that the tank and the aircraft would continue to be hugely important instruments on the post-1973 battlefield. At a symposium dedicated to the lessons of the Yom Kippur War, the IDF chief of staff during the war asserted that:

> The air force and armor remain the decisive factors on the battlefield. Their superiority and their success in battle are vital for victory in war. . . . In my opinion, the decisive role of the air force and the armor is true in defense and in offense.[6]

Hence, the Israeli defense establishment's decision to build up the IDF's air and armored forces, both quantitatively and qualitatively, in the post-1973 years.

Still, the Israeli defense establishment also absorbed the lesson that, on a battlefield saturated with sophisticated antitank and air defense weapons, tanks and aircraft would function more effectively and at lower cost to themselves as part of a combined arms team that incorporated sufficient artillery, infantry, engineering, and logistical forces. The internalization of this lesson is what spurred the Israeli defense establishment to acquire large numbers of self-propelled artillery tubes, large numbers of APCs equipped with mortars and machine guns, large quantities of antitank missiles and other infantry weapons, and large numbers of engineering and logistical vehicles in the wake of the Yom Kippur War.[7]

The Israeli defense establishment did not simply content itself with expanding the size and sophistication of the IDF's combat units and weapons systems, however. It also made great qualitative improvements to the IDF's entire command and control (C^2) system. The Yom Kippur War C^2 system, which had proven to be problematic, particularly on the Sinai front, was replaced with a far more sophisticated and robust command, control, communications, and intelligence (C^3I) system that not only improved the links between various headquarters—for example, between GHQ and area commands—but also improved the links between the ground forces, the air force, and the navy, the need of which constituted yet another lesson learned from the IDF's experience in the Yom Kippur War. Furthermore, the inclusion of advanced intelligence-collection systems, especially UAVs, afforded both senior and junior IDF officers with access to real-time, actionable intelligence data for the first time in the IDF's history.

War-fighting Doctrine Reforms

Like the IDF's force structure reforms in the post-1973 years, the IDF's war-fighting doctrinal reforms in the same years displayed both continuity and change. The Israeli defense establishment, on the one hand, remained committed to offensive maneuver warfare based first and foremost on the tank and the aircraft as the IDF's principal modus operandi at both the operational and tactical levels of war. On the other hand, however, armor and airpower would henceforward operate within the context of a traditional combined arms approach to warfare, one in which the IDF's artillery, infantry, and engineering forces would have much enhanced roles in comparison to those they filled in the pre-1973 years. At the aforementioned symposium, the IDF's wartime chief of staff summed up the Israeli defense establishment's philosophy moving forward:

> Combined operations and the combined task force present what I consider to be one of the major lessons to be learned on the tactical and [operational] levels. . . . [D]uring [the Yom Kippur War], we [i.e., the IDF] realized that combined operations have a growing importance in modern warfare, and are becoming a crucial factor for success in every single battle, in every campaign[,] and in every war. The reason for this is the development and variety of modern sophisticated weapons. For instance, the efficiency of anti-aircraft [sic] missile batteries has been proven during the [Yom Kippur] War. Because of the efficiency of the missiles, the task of our aircraft was complicated to a great

extent, and many new difficulties and problems were introduced. It is therefore necessary to use different and combined weapons systems.

Anti-tank [sic] missiles have also proved significantly effective in battle, although less so than the myth broadcast during the war. This does not in any way decrease the importance of tanks on the battlefield. On the other hand, there is no denying the fact that the missiles endanger tanks, and hinder their accomplishment of missions on targets defended by infantry. It is therefore mandatory to combine artillery support with every armor operation—this in order to neutralize anti-tank [sic] missiles and infantry as much as possible. There is also need for massive artillery support against the enemy's artillery, which represents a significant obstacle to the advance of armor.

An armor operation must be accompanied by infantry in order to prevent anti-tank [sic] activity mainly in those areas where the tanks' visibility and fire are limited. To these should be added engineering crews, to cope with minefields, ditches[,] and other obstacles which, due to modern trends in the development of engineering equipment, such as quick mine-laying, have become quite numerous.[8]

Integration and symmetry among combat arms would be the hallmark of IDF campaigns going forward.

Another important dimension of the IDF's war-fighting doctrine that displayed both continuity and change in the post-1973 years concerned the priorities of the IAF. On the one hand, the air force continued to stress the attainment of air superiority vis-à-vis both Arab air forces and integrated air defense systems (IADSs) as its primary endeavor; hence, its postwar build-up emphasized the development of capabilities to shoot down aircraft, attack air bases, and suppress air defenses, especially surface-to-air missile (SAM) batteries. Providing assistance to the IDF's ground forces, especially in the close air support (CAS) role, continued to be rather low on its list of priorities. This ordering of priorities had the backing of the IDF, despite its experience in the Yom Kippur War. In the words of the IDF's wartime chief of staff:

> The primary goal of the air force is to secure the skies throughout the country [i.e., over Israel] and above the combat forces....
>
> I see the air force's main role in the support of ground forces in interdiction—to achieve destruction of the enemy's military

infrastructure, cause havoc among troop movements[,] and, in one word, to paralyze the enemy forces. Even before 1973, I considered the subject of [CAS] the last priority task of the air force. I always believed that ground forces, secure from the enemy's air activity, should defeat enemy ground forces unaided. The [Yom Kippur War] reconfirmed my belief that [CAS] is costly in casualties, and that there is no positive ratio between relatively great losses and limited results.[9]

On the other hand, its experience in the Yom Kippur War made clear to the IAF that, in a future war, it might have to assist the ground forces before it achieved air superiority vis-à-vis Arab air forces and IADSs; therefore, it improved its capability to do so in the post-1973 years, particularly by establishing a substantial antitank helicopter force.[10] The IAF intended these helicopters to serve as "flying tanks" that could respond very quickly to an opponent's attack, using terrain-masking techniques to minimize their exposure to air defense weapons while knocking out tanks with their antitank missiles.

The status of the navy within the IDF's war-fighting doctrine evolved as well as a result of its experience in the Yom Kippur War. Before the war, the Israeli defense establishment had viewed the IN as little more than a coastal defense force whose contributions to the state's security were confined to preventing a seaborne attack and to keeping open the maritime routes to Israel, particularly those in the Mediterranean Sea, so that cargo could continue to flow into and out of Israeli ports. During the war, however, not only did the IN prevent attacks against targets on the Israeli coast and keep the Mediterranean shipping lanes open by sweeping the Egyptian and Syrian navies from the sea in a series of encounters between FPBs armed with antiship missiles, but it also helped to tie down significant Egyptian and Syrian army forces along their coasts, where they could not contribute to the fight against IDF ground forces, by carrying out attacks against strategic targets—for example, ports and POL facilities—along their coasts in loose coordination with the IAF.[11] Furthermore, in the Red Sea area, persistent IN attacks against Egyptian anchorages in the area helped the IDF's ground forces to conquer more territory during their cross-canal offensive than would have been possible without the navy's assistance. The IDF's wartime chief of staff summed up the Israeli defense establishment's newfound attitude after the war toward the IN:

> . . . I changed my mind about the tasks of the [IN] after the [Yom Kippur War]. My belief [before the war] was that our navy,

greatly outnumbered by the Arab navies, [had] only one task: to defend the coast. . . . Due to [its] excellent performance, I came to the conclusion that the [IN] can do much more in the event of another war.[12]

His comments would be amply validated during the next Arab–Israeli war, the 1982 Lebanon War.

The Test of War

Though not nearly as swift or spectacular as its victories in the 1956 Sinai Campaign, the 1967 Six-Day War, or even the Yom Kippur War, the IDF unquestionably defeated its opponents, the Palestine Liberation Organization (PLO) and the Syrian army, in the Lebanon War. And its force structure and war-fighting doctrinal reforms in the post-1973 years clearly made a significant contribution to this triumph. If not for the fact that much of the fighting occurred in urban or mountainous terrain, which imposed severe limits on how the IDF could wage war in these areas, it would have undoubtedly won a speedier and more lopsided victory.[13]

The IAF recorded one of the two most impressive achievements in its history when it destroyed the Syrian army's IADS in Lebanon's Bekaa Valley in very short order early on during hostilities.[14] Israel took the initiative in the Lebanon War, so the IAF had the opportunity to do what it had not had the opportunity to do during the Yom Kippur War: launch a dedicated, large-scale operation against its opponent's IADS. This operation saw the highly coordinated employment of UAVs as both real-time intelligence collectors and decoys, fighter-bombers equipped with different types of PGMs, airborne electronic warfare (AEW) and airborne warning and control system (AWACS) aircraft, and long-range artillery (gun and missile), all knit together by the most sophisticated C^3I battle management system in the world at that time. The IAF wiped out the Syrian IADS in the space of a few hours, with no losses to itself. When Syrian air force interceptors rose to challenge it, the IAF shot down up to 100, again with no losses to itself. With air superiority attained quickly at the beginning of the war, the IAF went on to furnish generally effective air support to the IDF's ground forces throughout the remainder of hostilities. The IAF's attack helicopter fleet proved itself to be a potent instrument in the antitank and CAS roles. Urban and mountainous terrain, however, often limited the amount of support that the IAF could deliver to the IDF's ground

CHAPTER 9

forces, particularly in built-up areas, as Israel sought to minimize collateral damage among the civilian populace.

The IDF deployed several division-sized combined arms task forces made up of tanks, mechanized and nonmechanized infantry, artillery, and engineers to fight PLO and Syrian forces in southern and eastern Lebanon, respectively. These combined arms task forces typically overcame PLO resistance in southern Lebanon rather easily, advancing to the outskirts of the Lebanese capital, Beirut, in about a week. The fighting against the Syrian army in eastern Lebanon proved more difficult and costly. Nevertheless, while driving the Syrian army back, the IDF eventually destroyed the equivalent of two Syrian armored divisions. Syrian tank losses were as much as 10 times higher than Israeli tank losses. Many Syrian tanks were put out of action by IDF infantry armed with antitank missiles. Though the IDF's task forces experienced occasional problems in coordinating their tanks, infantry, artillery, and engineering forces in battle, as well as some C^2 flaws, the generally efficient practice of combined arms warfare at both the operational and tactical levels contributed significantly to the IDF's defeat of PLO and Syrian forces in Lebanon.

Still, the Lebanon War is often viewed as a disaster in Israel, principally because of the prolonged and destructive siege of PLO forces in Beirut. It took several months of sustained IDF artillery bombardments and IAF air strikes to compel the PLO to abandon Lebanon altogether. The static, attritional nature of the fighting, which ran counter to the IDF's dominant ethos, in which substantial injury was inevitably inflicted on a civilian populace being used as a gigantic human shield by PLO forces, despite Israel's best efforts to minimize collateral damage, served to undermine in the minds of many Israelis what was otherwise a considerable military victory in the war.[15]

The IN also made a meaningful contribution to the IDF's triumph. Not only did it impose a blockade on Lebanon, ensuring that no arms reached its opponents via the sea, but it also provided effective naval artillery support via gunfire and missile salvo to IDF ground forces moving along the coast. And, most important of all, in a well-planned and well-executed combined operation with IDF ground forces, it landed an amphibious task force composed of tanks and parachute infantry behind PLO lines early in the war, facilitating the IDF's speedy advance toward Beirut.

Summary

The post-1973 intelligence, force structure, and war-fighting doctrinal reforms put in place by the Israeli defense establishment ensured that the IDF would remain more than a match for its Arab opponents. By the mid-1990s, however, Israel's strategic environment began to change dramatically from its strategic environment in the post-1973 years. Peace treaties with Egypt and Jordan, the virtually complete destruction of the Iraqi army in the 1991 Gulf War, and Syria's utter inability to achieve "strategic parity" with Israel overlapped with the steady rise of militarized nonstate actors like Hizbullah in Lebanon and Hamas in Judea, Samaria, and Gaza. The probability of interstate war between Israel and Arab states began to fall dramatically, while the probability of asymmetrical war between Israel and nonstate Arab actors began to rise just as dramatically. These complementary trends necessitated a thorough review of the IDF's force structure and war-fighting doctrine.

The Israeli defense establishment started to think in terms of a "smarter and slimmer" IDF. While it retains a commitment to offensive maneuver warfare to this day, as well as powerful mobile forces to conduct such warfare if necessary, the IDF has also undergone something of a paradigm shift over the past two decades. Its force structure and war-fighting doctrine have steadily shifted away from large-scale maneuver warfare in the direction of smaller-scale attrition warfare based on precision firepower, especially as a result of its experiences in three recent asymmetrical wars: the 2006 Second Lebanon War against Hizbullah, the 2008–9 Gaza War (commonly known as Operation Cast Lead) against Hamas (and allied groups), and the 2014 Gaza War (commonly known as Operation Protective Edge) against Hamas (and allied groups). For the foreseeable future, it seems, the IDF is likely to prepare itself primarily for battle against nonstate rather than state opponents.

Conclusion
From Defeat to Victory in the Yom Kippur War

In the years after the 1973 Yom Kippur War, Israelis suffered from a deep malaise whose origins lay in the war itself. One informed observer writing as late as the early 1990s noted that:

> The Yom Kippur War of October 1973 arouses an uncomfortable feeling among Israeli[s]. Many think of it as a disaster or a calamity. This is evident in references to the [w]ar in Israeli literature, or the way in which the [w]ar is recalled in the media, on the anniversary of its outbreak.[1]

In the years after Israel's spectacular victory in the 1967 Six-Day War, predictably enough, Israelis had come to believe that the Israel Defense Forces (IDF) could not possibly be caught unprepared for war. Nor did they envision a situation in which the IDF might actually face defeat on the battlefield. Yet, these nightmare scenarios transpired at the outset of the Yom Kippur War, shocking Israelis to the core. Add to these traumatic events the fact that it took three weeks—and the loss of over 2,500 soldiers and large quantities of fighting machines—for the IDF to reverse its initial setbacks in the Sinai and on the Golan and to once again best its Arab foes on the battlefield, and it is not hard to fathom why Israelis relate to the war with a sense of gloom and doom.

This perception notwithstanding, a very strong case can be made that the IDF performed better in the Yom Kippur War than in the Six-Day War, especially in light of the very different circumstances under which the two wars got underway. In 1967, not only did the IDF take the initiative, but it also had three weeks prior to the outbreak of hostilities to mobilize and deploy its regular and reserve forces, to give its reserves some refresher training, to update its intelligence files, to

CONCLUSION

prepare its fighting machines, and so on. In 1973, the IDF had none of these advantages. The Israeli government refused to grant permission for the Israel Air Force (IAF) to launch a preemptive strike, and the reserve component of the ground forces had not been readied for battle prior to the onset of hostilities. The IDF, put simply, went into battle cold, with almost no prewar preparation to speak of.

These crucial differences are too often forgotten by Israelis, who too often focus too intently on the mistakes that caused the setbacks of the opening days of hostilities and too little on the timely and effective improvisations that resulted in reversals of fortune on both fronts. Israelis too often focus, in other words, on how the war started rather than on how it finished, blowing these blunders out of proportion.

To be absolutely clear, the mistakes made prior to the Yom Kippur War by the IDF—as well as by the Israeli government, for that matter—were both very real and very debilitating. The IDF slanted both its force structure and war-fighting doctrine too heavily in favor of tanks and aircraft at the expense of infantry, artillery, engineers, and logistics. The IDF and the Israeli government greatly compounded these mistakes by not heeding numerous warning indicators, all of which pointed toward the outbreak of war in early October 1973. The IDF, consequently, had not mobilized and deployed its reserve forces, which constituted the bulk of its fighting power, to the Sinai and Golan fronts before the Egyptian and Syrian offensives got underway. The IDF's prewar operational plans for defending the fronts, therefore, immediately became moot, as its forces had to scramble to block the Egyptian and Syrian offensives. The abandonment of these plans had grave consequences for the IDF's tank corps and the IAF, both of which suffered heavy losses as a result and the latter of which could not provide effective ground support throughout much of the war.

To its enduring credit, the IDF recovered very swiftly from its initial setbacks. For reasons related to the natural and man-made topography, the quality and quantity of deployed forces, the efficiency of command and control (C^2), the speed of reserve mobilization, the application of airpower, and the employment of combined arms warfare, this turnaround occurred more quickly on the Golan than in the Sinai. Indeed, within two days of the outbreak of hostilities, the IDF had already begun a counterattack in the north to clear the Golan. A week later, after crushing an Egyptian advance toward the Sinai mountain passes by effectively employing combined arms warfare, including the application of airpower, the IDF began a counteroffensive across the Suez Canal. A few weeks after hostilities had begun, the IDF found itself within artillery range of the Syrian capital and a mere 100 kilometers from the Egyptian capital, the undisputed victor in the war. Its outstanding ability to extemporize under fire had led to one of the most spectacular battlefield reversals in the annals of warfare. And it accomplished this feat largely with the arms it had on hand before the war. American arms transfers during the war, while of political and psychological comfort to Israel, had no impact on the course of the fighting on the Golan front and only a limited impact on the Sinai front.

Israel did not fare nearly as well in the diplomatic arena during the Yom Kippur War. With the crucial exception of the United States, the world proved either openly hostile to its existence or, at best, utterly indifferent to its fate. Still, aside from maintaining its patron–client relationship with the United States, Israel did register a couple of diplomatic achievements during the war. First, it managed to arrive at an understanding with Jordan to limit the latter's participation in the fighting; thus, Israel never faced the prospect of war on three fronts simultaneously. And, second, Israel was able to refrain from activating its nuclear option during the war. Had it publicly brandished its nuclear arsenal, it is safe to assume, it would have suffered harmful diplomatic consequences, perhaps not least in its relationship with the United States.

During the Yom Kippur War, in sum, Israel moved from the precipice of catastrophic defeat to the edge of total victory in a matter of three weeks. That the IDF did not completely crush the Syrian and, especially, Egyptian armies can be attributed primarily to the involvement of the United States and the Soviet Union in the war, each in support of its own Middle Eastern agenda. Had they not inserted themselves into events surrounding the war, the IDF might well have won a more decisive victory in 1973 than it won in 1967. Any analysis of the Yom Kippur War must not lose sight of this salient point.

Notes

Introduction: The Historiography of the Yom Kippur War

1 The first four rounds were the 1947–9 War of Independence, the 1956 Sinai Campaign, the 1967 Six-Day War, when Israel captured the Sinai from Egypt and the Golan from Syria, and the 1969–70 War of Attrition.
2 Estimates of losses in the war, of course, vary from source to source; however, the numbers presented here represent widely accepted figures for both the Israelis and the Arabs. For aircraft losses, see Anthony H. Cordesman and Abraham R. Wagner, *The Lessons of Modern War (Volume I): The Arab–Israeli Conflicts, 1973–1989* (Boulder, CO: Westview Press, 1990), p. 89. For tank and artillery losses, see the chart presented by the first commander of the United States Army's Training and Doctrine (TRADOC) Command in "Implications of the Middle East War on U.S. Army Tactics, Doctrine, and Systems," in Richard M. Swain, Donald L. Gilmore, and Carolyn D. Conway, *Selected Papers of General William E. DePuy: First Commander, U.S. Army Training and Doctrine Command, 1 July 1973* (Fort Leavenworth, KS: U.S. Army Command and General Staff College, 1994), p. 79. And, for casualties, see Ze'ev Schiff, *A History of the Israeli Army: 1874 to the Present* (New York: Macmillan, 1985), p. 228.
3 See General DePuy's remark in "Implications of the Middle East War" in Swain, Gilmore, and Conway, *Selected Papers*, p. 77.
4 Dani Asher, "Time for the Next Generation," *Israel Defense*, No. 21 (July 2014), p. 98 cites a figure of 175 volumes in Hebrew as of mid-2014. This number has continued to grow in the following years.
5 Edward R. F. Sheehan, *The Arabs, Israelis, and Kissinger: A Secret History of American Diplomacy in the Middle East* (New York: Readers Digest Press, 1976), and Matti Golan, *The Secret Conversations of Henry Kissinger: Step-by-Step Diplomacy in the Middle East* (New York: Quadrangle, 1976).
6 Mohamed Heikal, *The Road to Ramadan* (New York: Ballantine Books, 1975), and Mohamed Heikal, *The October War* (New York: Crown, 1980).
7 William B. Quandt, *Decade of Decisions: American Policy Toward the Arab–Israeli Conflict, 1967–1976* (Berkeley: University of California Press,

NOTES TO INTRODUCTION

1977), and Michael Brecher, *Decisions in Crisis: Israel, 1967 and 1973* (Berkeley: University of California Press, 1980).
8 Alan Dowty, *Middle East Crisis: U.S. Decision Making in 1958, 1970, and 1973* (Berkeley: University of California Press, 1984); Steven L. Spiegel, *The Other Arab–Israeli Conflict: Making America's Middle East Policy, from Truman to Reagan* (Chicago: The University of Chicago Press, 1986); and Shlomo Aronson, *Conflict and Bargaining in the Middle East: An Israeli Perspective* (Baltimore: The Johns Hopkins University Press, 1978).
9 Victor Israelyan, *Inside the Kremlin During the Yom Kippur War* (University Park, PA: Pennsylvania State University Press, 1995).
10 Richard B. Parker (ed.), *The October War: A Retrospective* (Gainesville: University Press of Florida, 2001).
11 Moshe Gat, *In Search of a Peace Settlement: Egypt and Israel Between the Wars, 1967–1973* (New York: Palgrave Macmillan, 2012); Boaz Vanitek and Zaki Shalom, *The Nixon Administration and the Middle East Peace Process, 1969–1973: From the Rogers Plan to the Outbreak of the Yom Kippur War* (Brighton: Sussex Academic Press, 2013); and Yigal Kipnis, *1973: The Road to War* (Charlottesville, VA: Just World Books, 2013).
12 Craig Daigle, *The Limits of Détente: The United States, the Soviet Union, and the Arab–Israeli Conflict, 1969–1973* (New Haven: Yale University Press, 2012).
13 Nina Howland and Craig Daigle (eds.), *Foreign Relations of the United States, 1969–1976*, Volume XXV, *Arab–Israeli Crisis and War, 1973* (Washington, D.C.: United States Government Printing Office, 2011). Other volumes in the *FRUS* collection cover the years before and after the war.
14 Henry Kissinger, *Crisis: The Anatomy of Two Major Foreign Policy Crises* (New York: Simon and Schuster, 2004).
15 P. R. Kumaraswamy (ed.), *Revisiting the Yom Kippur War* (Oxford: Routledge, 2000).
16 Asaf Siniver (ed.), *The Yom Kippur War: Politics, Diplomacy, Legacy* (New York: Oxford University Press, 2013).
17 Ze'ev Schiff, *October Earthquake: Yom Kippur 1973* (Tel Aviv: University Publishing Projects, 1974), and Chaim Herzog, *The War of Atonement: October, 1973* (Boston: Little, Brown and Co., 1975).
18 Avraham (Bren) Adan, *On the Banks of the Suez: An Israeli General's Personal Account of the Yom Kippur War* (Novato, CA: Presidio Press, 1980).
19 Ariel Sharon (with David Chanoff), *Warrior: The Autobiography of Ariel Sharon* (New York: Simon and Schuster, 1990). This volume covers Sharon's entire life, not simply his wartime experience.
20 Hanoch Bartov, *Dado, 48 Years and 20 Days: The Full Story of the Yom Kippur War and the Man Who Led Israel's Army* (Tel Aviv: Maariv Book Guild, 1981).

21 Avigdor Kahalani, *The Heights of Courage: A Tank Leader's War on the Golan* (Westport, CT: Praeger, 1984).
22 Mohamed el Gamasy, *The October War: Memoirs of Field Marshal El Gamasy of Egypt* (Cairo: American University of Cairo Press, 1993); Saad el Shazly, *The Crossing of the Suez* (San Francisco: American Mideast Research, 1980); and Hassan el Badri, Taha el Magdoub, and Mohammed Dia el Din Zohdy, *The Ramadan War* (Fairfax, VA: HERO Books, 1978).
23 D. K. Palit, *Return to the Sinai: The Arab Offensive, October 1973* (New Dehli: Palit and Palit, 1974).
24 Dani Asher, *The Egyptian Strategy for the Yom Kippur War: An Analysis* (Jefferson, NC: McFarland, 2009).
25 Kenneth M. Pollack, *Arabs at War: Military Effectiveness, 1948–1991* (Lincoln: University of Nebraska Press, 2002).
26 Insight Team of the *London Sunday Times*, *The Yom Kippur War* (New York: Doubleday, 1974).
27 Edgar O'Ballance, *No Victor, No Vanquished: The Yom Kippur War* (Novato, CA: Presidio, 1978).
28 Trevor N. Dupuy, *Elusive Victory: The Arab–Israeli Wars, 1947–1974* (New York: Harper and Row, 1978).
29 Cordesman and Wagner, *The Lessons of Modern War*.
30 George W. Gawyrch, *The Albatross of Decisive Victory: War and Policy Between Egypt and Israel in the 1967 and 1973 Arab–Israeli Wars* (Westport, CT: Praeger, 2000).
31 Howard Blum, *The Eve of Destruction: The Untold Story of the Yom Kippur War* (New York: Harper, 2003).
32 Abraham Rabinovich, *The Yom Kippur War: The Epic Encounter that Transformed the Middle East* (New York: Schocken, 2004).
33 Simon Dunstan, *The Yom Kippur War: The Arab–Israeli War of 1973* (Oxford: Osprey Publishing, 2007).
34 Dani Asher et al., *Syrians at the Border: Strategies, Tactics, Battles, Israel's Northern Command, 1973* (Jerusalem: Contento de Semrik, 2014), and Emanuel Sakal, *Soldier in the Sinai: A General's Account of the Yom Kippur War* (Lexington, KY: University Press of Kentucky, 2014). Also see Dani Asher et al., *Inside Israel's Northern Command: The Yom Kippur War on the Syrian Border* (Lexington, KY: University Press of Kentucky, 2016), which is another version of *Syrians at the Border*.
35 Ori Orr, *These Are My Brothers: A Dramatic Story of Heroism During the Yom Kippur War* (Jerusalem: Contento de Semrik, 2013).
36 Central Intelligence Agency. Directorate of Intelligence, *The 1973 Arab–Israeli War: Overview and Analysis of the Conflict* (Langley, VA: Central Intelligence Agency, 1975).
37 Ze'ev Almog, *Flotilla 13: Israeli Naval Commandos in the Red Sea, 1967–1973* (Annapolis, MD: Naval Institute Press, 2010), and Abraham

Rabinovich, *The Boats of Cherbourg: The Navy that Stole Its Own Boats and Revolutionized Naval Warfare* (New York: Henry Holt, 1988).

38 Shlomo Aloni, *Ghosts of Atonement: Israeli F-4 Operations During the Yom Kippur War* (Atglen, PA: Schiffer Publishing, 2015), and Ra'anan Weiss, *The Israeli AF in the Yom Kippur War: Facts and Figures* (Kfar Tavor: Isradecal, 2014).

39 Walter J. Boyne, *The Two O'Clock War: The 1973 Yom Kippur Conflict and the Airlift that Saved Israel* (New York: Thomas Dunne Books, 2002).

40 Itzhak Brook, *In the Sands of Sinai: A Physician's Account of the Yom Kippur War* (Seattle: CreateSpace, 2012).

41 Uri Bar-Joseph, *The Watchman Fell Asleep: The Surprise of Yom Kippur and Its Sources* (Albany: SUNY Press, 2005).

42 Aryeh Shalev, *Israel's Intelligence Assessment Before the Yom Kippur War: Disentangling Deception and Distraction* (Brighton: Sussex Academic Press, 2010).

Part I Diplomacy

1 The American–Israeli Relationship

1 For an example of the former, see Stephen M. Walt, *The Origins of Alliances* (Ithaca, NY: Cornell University Press, 1987). For an example of the latter, see Warren Bass, *Support Any Friend: Kennedy's Middle East and the Making of the U.S.–Israel Alliance* (New York: Oxford University Press, 2003).

2 Charles W. Kegley, Jr. and Gregory A. Raymond, *When Trust Breaks Down: Alliance Norms and World Politics* (Columbia, SC: University of South Carolina Press, 1990), p. 52. Similarly, Ole Holsti, P. Terrance Hopmann, and John D. Sullivan contend that "an alliance is a formal agreement between [or among] two or more nations to collaborate on national security issues" in Ole Holsti, P. Terrance Hopmann, and John D. Sullivan, *Unity and Disintegration in International Alliances* (New York: John Wiley & Sons, 1973), p. 4.

3 In the way in which it has actually functioned over time, the American–Israeli patron–client relationship, despite its informal nature, has been similar in one respect to a bilateral asymmetric alliance. Members of such an alliance incur different costs and derive different benefits from this type of arrangement. The weaker member receives security benefits from the stronger member at a certain cost to the weaker member's autonomy, while the stronger member receives autonomy benefits from the weaker member at a certain cost to the stronger member's security. Put another way, the weaker member cedes some of its freedom to pursue its own foreign policy agenda in order to strengthen its military capabilities, while the stronger member cedes some of its military capabilities in order to increase its freedom to pursue its own foreign policy agenda. See James D. Morrow, "Alliances and Asymmetry: An Alternative to the

Capability Aggregation Model of Alliances," *American Journal of Political Science*, Vol. 35, No. 4 (November 1991), pp. 904–933.
4 The most authoritative accounts of why Israel did not predict the outbreak of war, in spite of all of the information in its hands, can be found in Uri Bar-Joseph, *The Watchman Fell Asleep: The Surprise of Yom Kippur and Its Sources* (Albany, NY: State University of New York Press, 2005), and Aryeh Shalev, *Israel's Intelligence Assessment Before the Yom Kippur War: Disentangling Deception and Distraction* (Brighton: Sussex Academic Press, 2010).
5 For accounts of American and Israeli conduct in the war, see Michael Brecher, *Decisions in Crisis: Israel, 1967 and 1973* (Berkeley, CA: University of California Press, 1980), pp. 51–76, 171–229, and 286–324; David Pollock, *The Politics of Pressure: American Arms and Israeli Policy Since the Six Day War* (Westport, CT: Greenwood Press, 1982), pp. 157–216; and Steven L. Spiegel, *The Other Arab–Israeli Conflict: Making America's Middle East Policy, from Truman to Reagan* (Chicago: The University of Chicago Press, 1985), pp. 219–314.
6 On the American role in the Israeli government's decision to forgo a preemptive air attack, see Brecher, *Decisions in Crisis*, pp. 177–178, 187–188, and 197–201, and Pollock, *The Politics of Pressure*, pp. 170–172.
7 See the October 7, 1973 memorandum of conversation between Secretary of State Henry Kissinger and Israeli Chargé d'Affaires Mordechai Shalev in Subject–Numeric Files 70–73, Policy 27 Arab–Israel, Record Group 59, Department of State Records, National Archives.
8 See the October 7, 1973 memorandum of conversation between Kissinger and Israeli Ambassador Simcha Dinitz in Records of Henry Kissinger, 1973–77, Record Group 59, Department of State Records, Box 25 (Category C 1973 Arab–Israeli War), National Archives.
9 See the October 6, 1973 telegram from Kissinger to President Richard Nixon in Middle East War Memos and Miscellaneous (October 1–October 17, 1973), National Security Council (NSC) File, Nixon Presidential Materials, Box 664, National Archives.
10 See the October 7, 1973 memorandum of conversation between Kissinger and Shalev in Subject–Numeric Files 70–73, Policy 27 Arab–Israel, Record Group 59, Department of State Records, National Archives.
11 On the initial American response to Israel's arms requests, see Brecher, *Decisions in Crisis*, pp. 209 and 213–216, and Pollock, *The Politics of Pressure*, pp. 172–174. For the transfer of American arms in Israeli planes, see the October 7, 1973 memorandum of conversation between Kissinger and Dinitz in Records of Henry Kissinger, 1973–1977, Record Group 59, Department of State Records, Box 25 (Category C 1973 Arab–Israeli War), National Archives, and the October 9, 1973 memorandum of conversation between them in Subject–Numeric Files 70–73, Policy Israel–United States, Record Group 59, Department of State Records, National Archives.

12 On the "airlift" during the first week of the war, see Avraham Greenbaum, "The US Airlift to Israel in 1973 and Its Origins," *Israel Affairs*, Vol. 13, No. 1 (January 2007), pp. 131–140, and Zach Levey, "Anatomy of an Airlift: United States Military Assistance to Israel During the 1973 War," *Cold War History*, Vol. 8, No. 4 (November 2008), pp. 481–501, especially pp. 485–488.
13 See the October 15, 1973 minutes of Kissinger's staff meeting in Transcripts of Secretary of State Kissinger's Staff Meetings, 1973–77, Record Group 59, Department of State Records, Box 1 (Secretary's Analytical Staff Meetings), National Archives.
14 See the October 21, 1973 telegram from Kissinger to General Brent Scowcroft, his deputy, in Henry A. Kissinger Trip–Moscow, Tel Aviv, London (October 20–October 23, 1973), Henry Kissinger Office Files, Nixon Presidential Materials, Box 39, National Archives, and the October 22 memorandum of conversation between Kissinger and Prime Minister Golda Meir in Subject–Numeric Files 70–73, Policy 7 United States–Kissinger, Record Group 59, Department of State Records, National Archives.
15 On American objections to the destruction of the Third Army, see Brecher, *Decisions in Crisis*, pp. 226–227, 296–298, and 302–304, and Pollock, *The Politics of Pressure*, pp. 177–178. To get a flavor of the discussions that took place between the United States and Israel on this issue, see the November 1, 1973 memoranda of conversations among Kissinger, Nixon, and Meir in Records of Henry Kissinger, 1973–77, Record Group 59, Department of State Records, Box 2 (NODIS Action Memos, 1973–76), National Archives.
16 See the October 26, 1973 telephone conversation between Kissinger and Dinitz in Kissinger Telephone Conversations, Chronological File, Nixon Presidential Materials, Box 23, National Archives.
17 A high-ranking Soviet official, incidentally, later revealed that the Soviet Union had not given serious thought to direct military intervention on behalf of Egypt. Victor Israelyan, *Inside the Kremlin During the Yom Kippur War* (University Park, PA: Pennsylvania State University Press, 1995).
18 Abba Eban, *Personal Witness: Israel Through My Eyes* (New York: Putnam, 1992), p. 538.
19 For American pressure during these postwar talks, see Pollock, *The Politics of Pressure*, pp. 179–196.
20 Quoted in Spiegel, *The Other Arab–Israeli Conflict*, pp. 248–249.
21 See the October 23, 1973 briefing by Kissinger to his staff in Transcripts of Secretary of State Kissinger's Staff Meetings, 1973–77, Record Group 59, Department of State Records, Box 1 (Secretary's Analytical Staff Meetings), National Archives.
22 See the October 14, 1973 telephone conversation between Nixon and Kissinger in Kissinger Telephone Conversations, Chronological File, Nixon Presidential Materials, Box 23, National Archives.

23 See the October 17, 1973 memorandum of conversation between Nixon and his advisors in Washington Special Actions Group Principles: Middle East War (October 17), NSC Institutional File, Box H–92 (Folder 6), National Archives.
24 Though calling for a preemptive attack in order to improve its prospects at the outset of the war, the IDF had also assured the government that Israel would eventually emerge victorious no matter which side fired the opening salvo. The IDF's confidence that it would win the war under any set of circumstances served to buttress the Israeli government's reasoning that Israel was correct to surrender to American pressure on the issue of a preemptive strike.
25 Moshe Dayan, *Moshe Dayan: Story of My Life* (New York: Warner Books, 1976), p. 556.
26 Quoted in Brecher, *Decisions in Crisis*, p. 181.

2 The Israeli-Jordanian Relationship

1 For an authoritative account of the Six-Day War, including Jordan's conduct before and during the fighting, see Michael B. Oren, *Six Days of War: June 1967 and the Making of the Modern Middle East* (New York: Oxford University Press, 2002).
2 Jordan's role in the Yom Kippur War is succinctly recounted in Chaim Herzog, *The War of Atonement: October, 1973* (Boston: Little, Brown and Co., 1975), pp. 139–142, and Abraham Rabinovich, *The Yom Kippur War: The Epic Encounter that Transformed the Middle East* (New York: Schocken Books, 2004), pp. 433–434.
3 Rabinovich, *The Yom Kippur War*, pp. 433–434.
4 Ibid., p. 434.
5 For a concise account of Israel's role in defeating Palestinian–Syrian forces, see Paul K. Huth, *Extended Deterrence and the Prevention of War* (New Haven: Yale University Press, 1988), pp. 86–97.
6 See the undated memorandum from the President's Assistant for National Security Affairs (or National Security Advisor) Henry Kissinger to President Richard Nixon in Nixon Presidential Materials, NSC Files, Kissinger Office Files, Box 137, Country Files, Middle East, Jordan/Rifai, National Archives, and the May 25 memorandum from National Security Council (NSC) member Harold Saunders to Kissinger, Nixon Presidential Materials, NSC Files, Box 618, Country Files, Middle East, Jordan, IX, January–October 1973, National Archives. For the Israeli–Jordanian meetings, see also Aryeh Shalev, *Israel's Intelligence Assessment Before the Yom Kippur War: Disentangling Deception and Distraction* (Brighton: Sussex Academic Press, 2010), pp. 78–88 and 262. The precise dates of some of the meetings are in dispute, but when exactly they took place is not important in the context of this chapter.

7 The substance of this meeting is described in Shalev, *Israel's Intelligence Assessment*, pp. 78–88. On the meeting, see also Uri Bar-Joseph, *The Watchman Fell Asleep: The Surprise of Yom Kippur and Its Sources* (Albany: The State University of New York Press, 2005).

8 See the October 8 telegram from the Embassy in Jordan to the Department of State, Nixon Presidential Materials, NSC Files, Box 618, Country Files, Middle East, Jordan, IX, January–October 1973, National Archives, and the October 8 minutes of the Washington Special Actions Group (WSAG) meeting, Nixon Presidential Materials, NSC Files, NSC Institutional Files (H–Files), Box H–117, Minutes Files, WSAG Meeting Minutes, Originals, 1973, National Archives.

9 See the October 9 memorandum of conversation among WSAG members, National Security Advisor, Memoranda of Conversation, Box 2, Ford Library; the October 9 telegram from the Embassy in Jordan to the Department of State, Nixon Presidential Materials, NSC Files, Box 618, Country Files, Middle East, Jordan, IX, January–October 1973, National Archives; and the October 10 memorandum from NSC staffer Helmut Sonnenfeldt to Secretary of State Kissinger, Nixon Presidential Materials, NSC Files, Kissinger Office Files, Box 68, Country Files, Europe, USSR, Dobrynin/Kissinger, Vol. 19 (July 13, 1973–Oct. 11, 1973), National Archives.

10 See the October 10 and 11 telegrams from the Embassy in Jordan to the Department of State, Nixon Presidential Materials, NSC Files, Box 618, Country Files, Middle East, Jordan, IX, January–October 1973, National Archives.

11 See the October 11 telegram from the Embassy in Jordan to the Department of State, Nixon Presidential Materials, NSC Files, Box 1174, Harold Saunders Files, Middle East Negotiations Files, 1973 Middle East War, 11 October 1973, File No. 6, National Archives.

12 See the October 9 and 10 telegrams from the Embassy in Jordan to the Department of State, Nixon Presidential Materials, NSC Files, Box 618, Country Files, Middle East, Jordan, IX, January–October 1973, National Archives.

13 For the existence of a direct Israeli–Jordanian communications channel, see the October 11 memorandum to Kissinger, Nixon Presidential Materials, NSC Files, Kissinger Office Files, Box 137, Country Files, Middle East, Jordan/Rifai, National Archives, and the October 12–13 memorandum of conversation between American and Israeli officials, Kissinger Papers, Box TS 33, Geopolitical File, Middle East, Middle East War Chronological File, 9–15 Oct. 1973, Library of Congress, Manuscript Division.

14 See the October 8, 10, and 11 telegrams from the Embassy in Jordan to the Department of State, Nixon Presidential Materials, NSC Files, Box 618, Country Files, Middle East, Jordan, IX, January–October 1973, National Archives, and Nixon Presidential Materials, NSC Files, Box

NOTES TO CHAPTER 2

   1174, Harold Saunders Files, Middle East Negotiations Files, 1973 Middle East War, 11 October 1973, File No. 6, National Archives.
15 See the October 8 and 9 telegrams from the Embassy in Jordan to the Department of State, Nixon Presidential Materials, NSC Files, Box 618, Country Files, Middle East, Jordan, IX, January–October 1973, National Archives.
16 See the October 8, 9, and 11 telegrams from the Embassy in Jordan to the Department of State, Nixon Presidential Materials, NSC Files, Box 618, Country Files, Middle East, Jordan, IX, January–October 1973, National Archives, and Nixon Presidential Materials, NSC Files, Box 1174, Harold Saunders Files, Middle East Negotiations Files, 1973 Middle East War, 11 October 1973, File No. 6, National Archives. Also see the October 9 memorandum of conversation among WSAG members, National Security Advisor, Memoranda of Conversation, Box 2, Ford Library.
17 See the October 8 and 9 telegrams from the Embassy in Jordan to the Department of State, Nixon Presidential Materials, NSC Files, Box 618, Country Files, Middle East, Jordan, IX, January–October 1973, National Archives.
18 See the October 10 telegram from the Embassy in Jordan to the Department of State, Nixon Presidential Materials, NSC Files, Box 618, Country Files, Middle East, Jordan, IX, January–October 1973, National Archives.
19 See the October 10 and 11 telegrams from the Embassy in Jordan to the Department of State, Nixon Presidential Materials, NSC Files, Box 618, Country Files, Middle East, Jordan, IX, January–October 1973, National Archives.
20 See the October 11 transcript of a telephone conversation between Kissinger and Soviet Ambassador to the United States Anatoly Dobrynin, Nixon Presidential Materials, Kissinger Telephone Conversations, Transcripts (Telcons), Anatoly Dobrynin File, Box 28, National Archives; the October 11 memorandum to Kissinger, Nixon Presidential Materials, NSC Files, Kissinger Office Files, Box 137, Country Files, Middle East, Jordan/Rifai, National Archives; and the October 12 transcript of a telephone conversation between Nixon and Kissinger, Nixon Presidential Materials, Kissinger Telephone Conversations, Transcripts (Telcons), Chronological File, Box 23, National Archives.
21 See the October 12 and 13 telegrams from the Embassy of Jordan to the Department of State, Nixon Presidential Materials, NSC Files, Box 618, Country Files, Middle East, Jordan, IX, January–October 1973, National Archives. Incidentally, Hussein also gave permission for Saudi Arabian troops in Jordan to move into Syria at the same time.
22 See the October 15 telegram from the Department of State to the Embassy in Jordan, Nixon Presidential Materials, NSC Files, Box 618, Country Files, Middle East, Jordan, IX, January–October 1973, National Archives.
23 For descriptions of these encounters, see Dani Asher et al., *Syrians at the*

NOTES TO CHAPTER 3

Border; Strategies, Tactics, Battles, Israel's Northern Command, 1973 (Jersualem: Contento de Semrik, 2014), ch. 13; Herzog, *The War of Atonement*, pp. 139–142; and Rabinovich, *The Yom Kippur War*, pp. 433–434.

24 See the minutes of the October 19 WSAG meeting, Nixon Presidential Materials, NSC Files, NSC Institutional Files (H–Files), Box H–117, WSAG Meetings Minutes, Originals, 1973, National Archives. Emblematic of Arab disorganization is the fact that Saudi Arabian forces moving out of Jordan got lost on their way to the Golan front, prompting the dispatch of Jordanian scouts to find them and then to lead them "out of the wilderness" to the battlefield.

25 See the October 21 telegram from Kissinger to the Embassy in Jordan, Nixon Presidential Materials, NSC Files, Box 772, Country Files, Europe, USSR, Vol. XXIX (May 1973–22 Oct. 1973), National Archives.

26 Asher et al. *Syrians at the Border*, ch. 13.

27 See the telegram from the Embassy in Jordan to the Department of State, Nixon Presidential Materials, NSC Files, Box 618, Country Files, Middle East, Jordan, IX, January–October 1973, National Archives. The Iraqis, always the most militant of Israel's foes, had indicated that they would not abide by any cease-fire agreement, and they were pushing the Syrians incessantly to reject it.

3 Nuclear Arms, Deterrence, and Compellence

1 Avner Cohen, *Israel and the Bomb* (New York: Columbia University Press, 1998), pp. 273–274.

2 Among the better recent histories of Israel's nuclear program are Cohen, *Israel and the Bomb*; Avner Cohen, *The Worst-kept Secret: Israel's Bargain with the Bomb* (New York: Columbia University Press, 2010); and Michael Karpin, *The Bomb in the Basement: How Israel Went Nuclear and What that Means for the World* (New York: Simon and Schuster, 2006).

3 On the connection between Israel's nuclear arms program and American arms assistance during the 1960s, see Warren Bass, *Support Any Friend: Kennedy's Middle East and the Making of the U.S.–Israel Alliance* (New York: Oxford University Press, 2003); Abraham Ben-Zvi, *John F. Kennedy and the Politics of Arms Sales to Israel* (London: Routledge, 2002); Abraham Ben-Zvi, *Lyndon B. Johnson and the Politics of Arms Sales to Israel: In the Shadow of the Hawk* (London: Routledge, 2004); and David Rodman, *Arms Transfers to Israel: The Strategic Logic Behind American Military Assistance* (Brighton: Sussex Academic Press, 2007), pp. 13–52.

4 Avner Cohen and William Burr, "Israel Crosses the Nuclear Threshold," *Bulletin of the Atomic Scientists*, Vol. 62, No. 3 (May 2006), pp. 22–30.

5 To deter an opponent is to prevent it from initiating an action that it would otherwise take in the absence of threats to impose potential costs in response to the action that outweigh any potential benefits that could

accrue to the opponent as a result of the action. For a thorough discussion of the concept of deterrence, see Thomas C. Schelling, *Arms and Influence* (New Haven: Yale University Press, 1966).

6 Shlomo Aronson (with Oded Brosh), *The Politics and Strategy of Nuclear Weapons in the Middle East: Opacity, Theory, and Reality, 1960–1991* (Albany: State University of New York Press, 1992), p. 147.

7 Aronson, *The Politics and Strategy of Nuclear Weapons*, indicates that Israel should adopt an overt nuclear posture, while Martin van Creveld, *Nuclear Proliferation and the Future of Conflict* (New York: The Free Press, 1993), believes that nuclear arms proliferation in the Middle East would help to stabilize the region.

8 Compellence is the opposite of deterrence. To compel an opponent is to coerce it into initiating an action that it would otherwise not take in the absence of threats to impose potential costs in response to inaction that outweigh any potential benefits that could accrue to the opponent as a result of inaction. For a thorough discussion of the concept of compellence, see Schelling, *Arms and Influence*.

9 Seymour M. Hersh, *The Samson Option: Israel's Nuclear Arsenal and American Foreign Policy* (New York: Random House, 1991), ch. 17.

10 Perhaps the best deconstructions of this nonevent are Elbridge Colby et al., *The Israeli "Nuclear Alert" of 1973: Deterrence and Signaling in Crisis* (Alexandria, VA: CNA, 2013), and Adam Raz, "The Significance of the Reputed Yom Kippur War Nuclear Affair," *Strategic Assessment*, Vol. 16, No. 4 (January 2014), pp. 103–118.

11 Ibid., especially pp. 103–106.

12 See the October 15 minutes of Secretary of State Henry Kissinger's staff meeting in Transcripts of Secretary of State Kissinger's Staff Meetings, 1973–77, Record Group 59, Department of State Records, Box 1 (Secretary's Analytical Staff Meetings), National Archives, and the October 23 staff meeting in Transcripts of Secretary of State Kissinger's Staff Meetings, 1973–77, Record Group 59, Department of State Records, Box 1 (Secretary's Analytical Staff Meetings), National Archives.

13 Victor Israelyan, *Inside the Kremlin During the Yom Kippur War* (University Park, PA: Pennsylvania State University Press, 1995).

14 See the October 26 telephone conversation between Kissinger and White House Chief of Staff Alexander Haig in Nixon Presidential Materials, Kissinger Telephone Conversations, Transcripts (Telcons), Chronological File, Box 23, National Archives.

15 See, for example, Yona Bendman and Yishai Cordova, "The Soviet Nuclear Threat Towards the Close of the Yom Kippur War," *The Jerusalem Journal of International Relations*, Vol. 5, No. 1 (March 1980), pp. 94–110.

NOTES TO CHAPTER 4

Part II Battle
4 Israeli Combined Arms Warfare

1. Anthony H. Cordesman and Abraham R. Wagner, *The Lessons of Modern War (Volume 1): The Arab–Israeli Conflicts, 1973–1989* (Boulder, CO: Westview Press, 1990), p. 54.
2. Robert S. Bolia, "Overreliance on Technology in Warfare: The Yom Kippur War as a Case Study," *Parameters*, Vol. 34, No. 2 (Summer 2004), pp. 51–52.
3. Emanuel Sakal, *Soldier in the Sinai: A General's Account of the Yom Kippur War* (Lexington, KY: University Press of Kentucky, 2014), p. 305.
4. For the distinction between the operational and tactical levels of warfare, see Edward N. Luttwak, *Strategy: The Logic of War and Peace* (Cambridge, MA: Harvard University Press, 1987), pp. 82–112.
5. United States Army. Department of Army Headquarters, *Army Doctrine Reference Publication No. 3-0: Unified Land Operations* (Washington, D.C.: Department of the Army Headquarters, 2012), p. 1–14. For a concise, jargon-free review of the concept, see Jonathan M. House, *Combined Arms Warfare in the Twentieth Century* (Lawrence, KS: University Press of Kansas, 2001), pp. 1–11.
6. Maneuver warfare privileges mobility over firepower in order to bring about the defeat of an enemy. Attrition warfare, on the other hand, privileges firepower over mobility to achieve the same objective.
7. On the tank buildup, see Sakal, *Soldier in the Sinai*, p. 98. On the aircraft buildup, see Central Intelligence Agency. Directorate of Intelligence, *The 1973 Arab–Israeli War: Overview and Analysis of the Conflict* (Langley, VA: Central Intelligence Agency, 1975), p. 28 and John F. Kreis, *Air Warfare and Air Base Air Defense* (Washington, D.C.: United States Government Printing Office, 1988), pp. 308 and 322. The CIA report was declassified in mid-2012. On the growth of the IAF's striking power, see Martin van Creveld, "Israel: Maneuver Warfare, Air Power, and Logistics," in Martin Van Creveld, Steven L. Canby, and Kenneth Brower, *Air Power and Maneuver Warfare* (Maxwell Air Force Base, AL: Air University Press, 1994), pp. 153–192.

    Parenthetically, numbers of men and machines—whether in reference to orders of battle, deployments for battle, or losses in battle—vary from source to source, sometimes significantly. The author has adopted the most plausible numbers throughout.
8. Sakal, *Soldier in the Sinai*, pp. 326–327.
9. Cordesman and Wagner, *The Lessons of Modern War*, p. 55, and Sakal, *Soldier in the Sinai*, pp. 100–102.
10. Sakal, *Soldier in the Sinai*, p. 98.
11. Cordesman and Wagner, *The Lessons of Modern War*, pp. 103–104, and Sakal, *Soldier in the Sinai*, p. 102.
12. For extensive treatments of the assumptions underlying "the concept,"

see Dani Asher, *The Egyptian Strategy for the Yom Kippur War: An Analysis* (Jefferson, NC: McFarland, 2009); Uri Bar-Joseph, *The Watchman Fell Asleep: The Surprise of Yom Kippur and Its Sources* (Albany: SUNY Press, 2005); and Aryeh Shalev, *Israel's Intelligence Assessment Before the Yom Kippur War: Disentangling Deception and Distraction* (Brighton: Sussex Academic Press, 2010).

13 The Yom Kippur War has not lacked for chroniclers over the years. Among the many general histories of the war, two of the best are: Chaim Herzog, *The War of Atonement: October, 1973* (Boston: Little, Brown and Co., 1975), and Abraham Rabinovich, *The Yom Kippur War: The Epic Encounter that Transformed the Middle East* (New York: Schocken, 2004).

14 For the force ratios on the Golan, see Directorate of Intelligence, *The 1973 Arab–Israeli War*, p. 53; Dani Asher et al., *Syrians at the Border: Strategies, Tactics, Battles, Israel's Northern Command, 1973* (Jerusalem: Contento de Semrik, 2014), chs. 1 and 5; Herzog, *The War of Atonement*, pp. 60–63; and Rabinovich, *The Yom Kippur War*, p. 142. (The author consulted an electronic version of Asher et al.'s volume, so the citations reference chapters rather than pages.)

15 For the force ratios in the Sinai, see Directorate of Intelligence, *The 1973 Arab–Israeli War*, pp. 74–78; Herzog, *The War of Atonement*, pp. 150–151; Rabinovich, *The Yom Kippur War*, p. 55; and Sakal, *Soldier in the Sinai*, p. 77.

16 Asher et al., *Syrians at the Border*, chs. 1 and 5; Directorate of Intelligence, *The 1973 Arab–Israeli War*, pp. 52–53; Herzog, *The War of Atonement*, pp. 60–63; and Rabinovich, *The Yom Kippur War*, p. 142.

17 The IDF's defensive stand against the Syrian onslaught is traced in Asher et al., *Syrians at the Border*, chs. 6–11; Directorate of Intelligence, *The 1973 Arab–Israeli War*, pp. 54–64; Herzog, *The War of Atonement*, pp. 78–127; and Rabinovich, *The Yom Kippur War*, pp. 142–175 and 187–216.

18 On the role and conduct of the IDF's Golan strongpoints, see Asher et al., *Syrians at the Border*, chs. 6–11.

19 Ori Orr, *These Are My Brothers: A Dramatic Story of Heroism During the Yom Kippur War* (Jerusalem: Contento de Semrik, 2013), furnishes a firsthand account of the rapid mobilization and deployment of IDF reserve forces on the Golan front.

20 Asher et al., *Syrians at the Border*, chs. 17 and 18 describe the contributions of artillery and engineering forces, respectively, on the Golan front.

21 Ibid., ch. 19 describes the IAF's contribution on the Golan front.

22 For the IDF's offensive into Syria and the fighting until the war's end, see Asher et al., *Syrians at the Border*, chs. 12–14; Directorate of Intelligence, *The 1973 Arab–Israeli War*, pp. 64–68; Herzog, *The War of Atonement*, pp. 128–145; and Rabinovich, *The Yom Kippur War*, pp. 284–318.

23 Directorate of Intelligence, *The 1973 Arab–Israeli War*, p. 65.

24 On the recapture of the Mount Hermon strongpoint, see Asher et al.,

NOTES TO CHAPTER 4

Syrians at the Border, ch. 14; Herzog, *The War of Atonement*, pp. 143–144; and Rabinovich, *The Yom Kippur War*, pp. 446–457.

25 Herzog, *The War of Atonement*, p. 151; Rabinovich, *The Yom Kippur War*, p. 55; and Sakal, *Soldier in the Sinai*, pp. 467–470.

26 On tank losses on the southern front during the first day of war, see Rabinovich, *The Yom Kippur War*, p. 233, and Sakal, *Soldier in the Sinai*, p. 174.

27 For the October 8 counterattack, see John J. McGrath, "Sinai 1973: Israeli Maneuver Organization and the Battle of the Chinese Farm," in John J. McGrath (ed.), *An Army at War: Change in the Midst of Conflict* (Fort Leavenworth, KS: U.S. Army Command and General Staff College, 2005), pp. 67–68, and, especially, Sakal, *Soldier in the Sinai*, pp. 208–284.

28 McGrath, "Sinai 1973," p. 65, and Sakal, *Soldier in the Sinai*, p. 246.

29 Sakal, *Soldier in the Sinai*, pp. 208–284.

30 McGrath, "Sinai 1973," p. 69, and Sakal, *Soldier in the Sinai*, p. 300.

31 Directorate of Intelligence, *The 1973 Arab–Israeli War*, p. 89.

32 On the battle and the losses, see Directorate of Intelligence, *The 1973 Arab–Israeli War*, pp. 89–90; Herzog, *The War of Atonement*, pp. 205–207; Rabinovich, *The Yom Kippur War*, pp. 353–355; and Sakal, *Soldier in the Sinai*, pp. 302–304.

33 Treatments of the crossing operation can be found in Directorate of Intelligence, *The 1973 Arab–Israeli War*, pp. 91–97; Herzog, *The War of Atonement*, pp. 208–230; McGrath, "Sinai 1973," pp. 63–109; and Rabinovich, *The Yom Kippur War*, pp. 358–399.

34 For the IDF advance into Egypt, see Directorate of Intelligence, *The 1973 Arab–Israeli War*, pp. 97–99; Herzog, *The War of Atonement*, pp. 231–250; and Rabinovich, *The Yom Kippur War*, pp. 416–477.

35 For the IAF's prewar thinking, see Rabinovich, *The Yom Kippur War*, pp. 32–34, and Sakal, *Soldier in the Sinai*, pp. 328–333.

36 On American pressure to refrain from a preemptive strike, see the October 6, 1973 telegram from Secretary of State Henry Kissinger to President Richard Nixon in Middle East War Memos and Miscellaneous (October 1–October 17), National Security Council (NSC) File, Nixon Presidential Materials, Box 664, National Archives, and the October 7, 1973 memorandum of conversation between Kissinger and Israeli Ambassador to the United States Simcha Dinitz in Records of Henry Kissinger, 1973–1977, Record Group 59, State Department Records, Box 25 (Category C 1973 Arab–Israeli War), National Archives. Also see Michael Brecher, *Decisions in Crisis: Israel, 1967 and 1973* (Berkeley: University of California Press, 1980), pp. 177–178, 187–188, and 197–201.

37 Steven J. Rosen and Martin Indyk, "The Temptation to Pre-empt in a Fifth Arab–Israeli War," *Orbis*, Vol. 20, No. 3 (Summer 1976), pp. 271–272.

38 John R. Carter, *Airpower and the Cult of the Offensive* (Maxwell Air Force Base, AL: Air University Press, 1998), pp. 52–65.

39 In a conversation with the author on June 25, 2007 at the Israel Air Force Center (IAFC), Herzliya, Israel, Brigadier General (Ret.) Itzhak Amitay, who flew many combat missions on the southern front during the Yom Kippur War, confirmed that this operation had made progress before it was scrubbed by IDF GHQ. For summaries of this operation, see Rabinovich, *The Yom Kippur War*, pp. 175–180, and Sakal, *Soldier in the Sinai*, pp. 338–342.
40 Rabinovich, *The Yom Kippur War*, pp. 178–179, and Sakal, *Soldier in the Sinai*, pp. 338-342.
41 For a summary and assessment of IAF activity in the Yom Kippur War, see David Rodman, *Sword and Shield of Zion: The Israel Air Force in the Arab–Israeli Conflict, 1948–2012* (Brighton: Sussex Academic Press, 2013), pp. 31–38.
42 Sakal, *Soldier in the Sinai*, pp. 384–387.
43 Cordesman and Wagner, *The Lessons of Modern War*, pp. 94–95, and Sakal, *Soldier in the Sinai*, pp. 396–398.
44 William E. DePuy, "Letter to Senator John C. Culver from General DePuy, 12 May 1975," in Richard M. Swain, Donald L. Gilmore, and Carolyn D. Conway, *Selected Papers of General William E. DePuy: First Commander, U.S. Army Training and Doctrine Command, 1 July 1973* (Fort Leavenworth, KS: U.S. Army Command and General Staff College, 1994), p. 166.

5 Israeli Resurgence on the Golan versus in the Sinai

1 For the width of the Syrian penetration, see Central Intelligence Agency. Directorate of Intelligence, *The 1973 Arab–Israeli War: Overview and Analysis of the Conflict* (Langley, VA: Central Intelligence Agency, 1975), p. 62.
2 For the width of the Egyptian bridgeheads, see ibid., p. 83.
3 Ibid., p. 51.
4 Chaim Herzog, *The War of Atonement: October, 1973* (Boston: Little, Brown and Co., 1975), p. 155, and Abraham Rabinovich, *The Yom Kippur War: The Epic Encounter that Transformed the Middle East* (New York: Schocken, 2004), p. 136. This number does not include the hundreds of Egyptian special forces troops lost in abortive attempts to infiltrate behind IDF lines via helicopter.
5 On the Bar Lev Line, see Rabinovich, *The Yom Kippur War*, p. 18, and Emanuel Sakal, *Soldier in the Sinai: A General's Account of the Yom Kippur War* (Lexington, KY: University Press of Kentucky, 2014), pp. 47 and 467–468. The IDF also had a string of strongpoints set well back from the Suez Canal, which were not part of this line. These positions played no direct role in the IDF's defensive stand in the Sinai.
6 Directorate of Intelligence, *The 1973 Arab–Israeli War*, p. 86.
7 For the antitank ditch on the Golan in particular, and the IDF's man-made

obstacles in general, see Dani Asher et al., *Syrians at the Border: Strategies, Tactics, Battles, Israel's Northern Command, 1973* (Jersualem: Contento de Semrik, 2014), ch. 2, and Directorate of Intelligence, *The 1973 Arab–Israeli War*, p. 55. (The author consulted an electronic version of Asher et al.'s volume, so the citations reference chapters rather than pages.)

8 For the IDF tank deployment in the Sinai, see Sakal, *Soldier in the Sinai*, pp. 463 and 467–468.
9 For the IDF tank deployment on the Golan, see Asher et al., *Syrians at the Border*, ch. 5.
10 Sakal, *Soldier in the Sinai*, p. 164.
11 Asher et al., *Syrians at the Border*, ch. 5.
12 On how the war initially unfolded in the Sinai, see Herzog, *The War of Atonement*, pp. 146–181; Rabinovich, *The Yom Kippur War*, pp. 101–141; and Sakal, *Soldier in the Sinai*, pp. 111–208.
13 On how the war initially unfolded on the Golan, see Asher et al., *Syrians at the Border*, chs. 6–11; Herzog, *The War of Atonement*, pp. 78–127; and Rabinovich, *The Yom Kippur War*, pp. 142–216 and 284–306.
14 For IDF C^2 in the Sinai and on the Golan, see Asher et al., *Syrians at the Border* and Sakal, *Soldier in the Sinai*. Sakal, who served as a tank battalion commander on the southern front during the war, offers a searing critique of Israeli C^2 problems in the Sinai in the first week of the war.
15 On the October 8 counterattack, see Herzog, *The War of Atonement*, pp. 182–196; Rabinovich, *The Yom Kippur War*, pp. 235–252; and Sakal, *Soldier in the Sinai*, pp. 208–284.
16 Directorate of Intelligence, *The 1973 Arab–Israeli War*, p. 16. On the shortage of tank transporters, see Sakal, *Soldier in the Sinai*, p. 102.
17 Ori Orr, *These Are My Brothers: A Dramatic Story of Heroism During the Yom Kippur War* (Jerusalem: Contento de Semrik, 2013), provides a first-hand account of the rapid mobilization and deployment of IDF reserve forces to the Golan front. Orr served as the commander of the first reserve tank brigade to reach the front during the war. Also see Asher et al., *Syrians at the Border*, chs. 6 and 8, on the mobilization and deployment of IDF reserve forces.
18 On American pressure to refrain from a preemptive strike, see the October 6, 1973 telegram from Secretary of State Henry Kissinger to President Richard Nixon in Middle East War Memos and Miscellaneous (October 1–October 17), National Security Council (NSC) File, Nixon Presidential Materials, Box 664, National Archives, and the October 7, 1973 memorandum of conversation between Kissinger and Israeli Ambassador to the United States Simcha Dinitz in Records of Henry Kissinger, 1973–1977, Record Group 59, State Department Records, Box 25 (Category C 1973 Arab–Israeli War), National Archives. Also see Michael Brecher, *Decisions in Crisis: Israel, 1967 and 1973* (Berkeley: University of California Press, 1980), pp. 177–178, 187–188, and 197–201.

19 Directorate of Intelligence, *The 1973 Arab–Israeli War*, p. 60, and Ra'anan Weiss, *The Israeli AF in the Yom Kippur War: Facts and Figures* (Kfar Tavor: Isradecal, 2014), p. 47.
20 Directorate of Intelligence, *The 1973 Arab–Israeli War*, p. 34.
21 Weiss, *The Israeli AF in the Yom Kippur War*, pp. 33, 47, 57, 65, 73, 81, and 89.
22 For a concise definition of combined arms warfare, see United States Army. Department of Army Headquarters, *Army Doctrine Reference Publication No. 3–0: Unified Land Operations* (Washington, D.C.: Department of the Army Headquarters, 2012), p. 1–14.
23 On the October 14 tank battle and the losses, see Directorate of Intelligence, *The 1973 Arab–Israeli War*, pp. 89–90; Herzog, *The War of Atonement*, pp. 205–207; Rabinovich, *The Yom Kippur War*, pp. 353–355; and Sakal, *Soldier in the Sinai*, pp. 302–304.
24 The hillier terrain inland from the Suez Canal also offered more in the way of concealment for IDF tanks, as well as afforded them high ground from which to pick off Egyptian tanks over great distances by employing their superior long-range gunnery.
25 Directorate of Intelligence, *The 1973 Arab–Israeli War*, p. 66.

6 Israeli Airpower in the Six-Day and Yom Kippur Wars

1 In the early years of the twenty-first century, the Israel Air Force (IAF) officially changed its name to the Israel Air and Space Force (IASF) in order to reflect the fact that it now operates in space as well. Nevertheless, this chapter shall refer to the IAF, as the historical events described and analyzed herein occurred long before the adoption of the new name.
2 The author would like to thank United States Air Force (USAF) Lieutenant Colonel Paul D. Berg for his helpful comments about some of the terminology appearing in this chapter. Responsibility for any nontraditional and/or imprecise use of this terminology, of course, lies solely with the author.
3 Even though many of the IAF's air base attacks in both the 1967 and 1973 wars might well be characterized as strategic attacks, they will be discussed in this article under the rubric of air superiority, because the main intent of these attacks was to contribute to the attainment of Israeli air superiority.
4 A meticulous descriptive account of the preparation and execution of Operation Focus can be found in Shlomo Aloni, *The June 1967 Six-Day War (Volume A): Operation Focus* (Bat Hefer: Isradecal, 2008). His account relies on a combination of official IAF records and interviews with participating aircrews.
5 The standard air base attack sortie consisted of one bombing run to crater runways, followed by three strafing passes, primarily to destroy aircraft, but also to smash other targets of opportunity (e.g., heavy equipment and

maintenance workshops). E-mail communication, August 10, 2008, with Lieutenant Colonel (Ret.) Amos Cohen, who flew two air base attack sorties on June 5.
6   Aloni, *The June 1967 Six-Day War*, pp. 179–180.
7   Ibid., pp. 179–180.
8   Ibid., pp. 54 and 179.
9   These figures come from the IAF Historical Branch. They are taken from Kenneth M. Pollack, "Air Power in the Six-Day War," *The Journal of Strategic Studies*, Vol. 28, No. 3 (June 2005), pp. 471–503. For the figures, see the table on p. 478.
10 For a concise and trenchant examination of IAF CAS and interdiction attacks on each of the three fronts—the Sinai, the Judean and Samarian, and the Golan—see Pollack, "Air Power in the Six-Day War," pp. 477–485. On the Sinai front, also see Martin van Creveld, "Israel: Maneuver Warfare, Air Power, and Logistics," in Martin van Creveld, Steven L. Canby, and Kenneth S. Brower, *Air Power and Maneuver Warfare* (Maxwell Air Force Base, AL: Air University Press, 1994), pp. 153–192. For the Sinai front, see pp. 168–169.
11 For the conclusion that the IAF destroyed few tanks (on all three fronts), see the report by the Joint Technical Coordinating Group for Munitions Effectiveness, *Special Report: Survey of Combat Damage to Tanks*, Volumes I–III (Washington, D.C.: Defense Intelligence Agency, 1970). Also see Pollack, "Air Power in the Six-Day War," pp. 483–485 and van Creveld, "Israel," pp. 168–169.
12 For the specifics on the paratrooper landings, see the day-by-day synopsis of the Six-Day War on the official IAF web site, <www.iaf.org.il>.
13 van Creveld, "Israel," p. 168.
14 On American pressure to refrain from a preemptive strike, see the October 6, 1973 telegram from Secretary of State Henry Kissinger to President Richard Nixon in Middle East War Memos and Miscellaneous (October 1–October 17), National Security Council File, Nixon Presidential Materials, Box 664, National Archives, and the October 7, 1973 memorandum of conversation between Kissinger and Israeli Ambassador to the United States Simcha Dinitz in Records of Henry Kissinger, 1973–1977, Record Group 59, State Department Records, Box 25 (Category C 1973 Arab–Israeli War), National Archives. Also see Michael Brecher, *Decisions in Crisis: Israel, 1967 and 1973* (Berkeley: University of California Press, 1980), pp. 177–178, 187–188, and 197–201.
15 In a June 25, 2007 conversation with the author at the Israel Air Force Center, Herzliya, Israel, Brigadier General (Ret.) Itzhak Amitay, who flew many combat missions on the Sinai front during the war, confirmed that the IAF was making headway against the Egyptian IADS before IDF general headquarters (GHQ) scrubbed the operation. Also see Abraham Rabinovich, *The Yom Kippur War: The Epic Encounter that Transformed the Middle East* (New York: Schocken, 2004), pp. 175–180, and Emanuel

Sakal, *Soldier in the Sinai: A General's Account of the Yom Kippur War* (Lexington, KY: University Press of Kentucky, 2014), pp. 338–342.

16 See Anthony Cordesman and Abraham R. Wagner, *The Lessons of Modern War (Volume 1): The Arab–Israeli Conflicts, 1973–1989* (Boulder, CO: Westview Press, 1989), p.83. For a compact and insightful treatment of the aerial dimension of the Yom Kippur War, see pp. 73–102.

17 Ibid., p. 83. On the inept execution of Operation Model 5, see Ra'anan Weiss, *The Israeli AF in the Yom Kippur War: Facts and Figures* (Kfar Tavor: Isradecal, 2014), p. 38.

18 Cordesman and Wagner, *The Lessons of Modern War*, p. 90. Also see the October 22, 1973 memorandum of conversation between Kissinger and Israeli military and political leaders in Political Affairs and Relations, Arab–Israeli Conflict (27–14), Record Group 59, Subject–Numeric Files 70–73, National Archives. In this document, IAF commander Major General Binyamin Peled is quoted to the effect that Israel had lost more than 100 aircraft in the war to this point in time (i.e., a few days before the final cease-fire agreement took effect).

Parenthetically, on a per sortie basis, the overall IAF loss rate in the 1973 war was lower than the overall loss rate in the 1967 war. Though the IAF lost approximately 2.3 times as many aircraft in the Yom Kippur War, it flew about 3.5 times as many sorties in this conflict.

19 The official IAF web site claims 277 Arab aircraft shot down in air-to-air combat during the Yom Kippur War at a cost of only five Israeli aircraft. Many unofficial sources adopt somewhat higher figures for the number of Arab aircraft shot down as well as the number of Israeli aircraft lost in air battles.

20 Cordesman and Wagner, *The Lessons of Modern War*, p. 96.

21 Ibid., p. 90.

22 van Creveld, "Israel," p. 181.

23 Regardless of its name, the Bar Lev Line was not intended to hold off a large-scale Egyptian thrust across the Suez Canal. It consisted of a series of quite small and widely dispersed strongholds meant simply to protect Israeli troops from Egyptian army shelling and to provide the IDF with observation posts on the front line.

24 The IAF suffered about half of its total aircraft losses during the first few days of the war. See van Creveld, "Israel," p. 182.

25 On the growth in the IAF's firepower between the wars, see ibid., pp. 170–171 and 184.

26 For the generally poor performance of Egypt's air-to-ground missiles, see Cordesman and Wagner, *The Lessons of Modern War*, p. 98.

27 The fear of Israeli airpower may also have provided Jordan with the diplomatic cover that it required to refrain from attacking Israel from its own territory. Instead, the Jordanian army—and, for that matter, the Iraqi army—deployed forces to the Golan front to fight alongside the Syrian army.

28 The following paragraphs are intended only to illustrate the limits of the IAF's contribution to the ground campaigns in 1967 and 1973. A detailed assessment of the relative effectiveness of airpower versus ground power in these wars falls outside the scope of this chapter.

29 Sinai front divisional commander Major General Ariel Sharon, for example, opted to fight the crucial battle at Abu Agueila at night. Though the IAF did transport paratroopers behind Egyptian lines during this battle, the air force otherwise did not participate in it. On the Abu Agueila battle, see van Creveld, "Israel," p. 166.

30 Even highly knowledgeable observers have subscribed to this line of thinking. For a representative example, see the January 14, 1974 letter from General William E. DePuy, onetime head of the United States Army's Training and Doctrine (TRADOC) Command, to United States Army Chief of Staff General Creighton Abrams in the Orwin C. Talbott Papers, Deputy CG TRADOC, Arab–Israeli War (1973) Box, Letter from General DePuy to General Abrams Folder, United States Army Military History Institute.

31 The IAF lost about 20–25 aircraft in CAS and interdiction sorties during the Six-Day War. It lost about 70–75 aircraft in the same types of sortie during the Yom Kippur War. In light of the fact that the IAF flew roughly three times as many CAS and interdiction sorties in the 1973 war, not to mention that it flew them in the face of much more robust IADSs, its loss rate in this war for these types of mission would not seem to compare unfavorably with the one obtained in the 1967 war.

32 Some knowledgeable observers have given an affirmative answer to this question, while others have given a negative answer. For the former, see Steven J. Rosen and Martin Indyk, "The Temptation to Pre-empt in a Fifth Arab–Israeli War," *Orbis*, Vol. 20, No. 3 (Summer 1976), pp. 271–272. For the latter, see John R. Carter, *Airpower and the Cult of the Offensive* (Maxwell Air Force Base, AL: Air University Press, 1998), pp. 52–65.

33 For problems with the IAF's reconnaissance activities in the Yom Kippur War, see Cordesman and Wagner, *The Lessons of Modern War*, pp. 99–100.

34 Binyamin Peled, "The Air Force in the Yom Kippur War: Main Moves and Lessons," in Louis Williams (ed.), *Military Aspects of the Israeli–Arab Conflict* (Tel Aviv: University Publishing Projects, 1975), p. 240.

Part III Lessons

7 The Impact of American Arms Transfers to Israel

1 Abraham Rabinovich, *The Yom Kippur War: The Epic Encounter that Transformed the Middle East* (New York: Schocken, 2004), p. 491.

2 On how the American–Israeli relationship functioned during the Yom Kippur War, see David Rodman, *Arms Transfers to Israel: The Strategic*

NOTES TO CHAPTER 7

Logic Behind American Military Assistance (Brighton: Sussex Academic Press, 2007), pp. 76–83.

3   See the October 6 minutes of the Washington Special Actions Group (WSAG) meeting, Nixon Presidential Materials, National Security Council (NSC) Files, Kissinger Office Files, Box 129, Country Files, Middle East, National Archives. See also Zach Levey, "Anatomy of an Airlift: United States Military Assistance to Israel During the 1973 War," *Cold War History*, Vol. 8, No. 4 (November 2008), pp. 481–501, at p. 486.

4   Levey, "Anatomy of an Airlift," and Rodman, *Arms Transfers to Israel.*

5   Levey, "Anatomy of an Airlift," pp. 485–488. See also the October 8 memorandum from William Quandt and Donald Stukel of the NSC staff to Secretary of State Henry Kissinger, Nixon Presidential Materials, NSC Files, NSC Institutional Files (H–Files), Box H-93, Meeting Files (1969–1974), WSAG Meetings, National Archives; the October 9 memorandum of conversation between American and Israeli officials, RG 59, Records of Henry Kissinger: Lot 91 D 414, Box 25, Arab–Israeli War, National Archives; the October 9 memorandum of conversation among American officials, National Security Advisor, Memoranda of Conversation, Box 2, Ford Library; the October 9 memoranda of conversation between American and Israeli officials, RG 59, Central Files 1970–73 POL ISR–US, National Archives; and the October 11 transcript of a telephone conversation between Kissinger and the President's Deputy Assistant for National Security Affairs (Deputy National Security Advisor) Brent Scowcroft, Nixon Presidential Materials, Kissinger Telephone Conversations, Transcripts (Telcons), Chronological Files, Box 22, National Archives.

6   Officials in the State and Defense Departments later accused each other of deliberately delaying the establishment of an arms pipeline. See, for example, Avraham Greenbaum, "The US Airlift to Israel in 1973 and Its Origins," *Israel Affairs*, Vol. 13, No. 1 (January 2007), pp. 131–140, and Levey, "Anatomy of an Airlift," p. 482. On the American inability to secure civilian aircraft to transport munitions to Israel, see the October 12 transcript of a telephone conversation between President Richard Nixon and Kissinger, Nixon Presidential Materials, Kissinger Telephone Conversations, Transcripts (Telcons), Chronological File, Box 23, National Archives.

7   On the evolving progress and scope of the American air- and sealift, see Levey, "Anatomy of an Airlift," pp. 488–494. See also the many United States government documents—which are far too numerous to list individually—that trace developments related to the air- and sealift.

8   For the total amounts of arms shipped to Israel during and after the war, see Levey, pp. 481 and 494.

9   Numerous books chronicle the battlefield events of the Yom Kippur War. Among the best are Chaim Herzog, *The War of Atonement: October, 1973*

(Boston: Little, Brown and Co., 1975), and Rabinovich, *The Yom Kippur War*.

10 See the October 12–13 memorandum of conversation between American and Israeli officials, Kissinger Papers, Box TS 33, Geopolitical File, Middle East, Middle East War Chronological File, 9–15 Oct. 1973, Library of Congress, Manuscript Division, and the October 13 transcript of a telephone conversation between Kissinger and Secretary of Defense James Schlesinger, Nixon Presidential Materials, Kissinger Telephone Conversations, Transcripts (Telcons), Chronological File, Box 23, National Archives.

11 See the October 13 memorandum of conversation among WSAG members, National Security Advisor, Memoranda of Conversation, Box 2, Ford Library.

12 Avraham (Bren) Adan, *On the Banks of the Suez: An Israeli General's Personal Account of the Yom Kippur War* (Novato, CA: Presidio Press, 1980), p. 163.

13 Emanuel Sakal, *Soldier in the Sinai: A General's Account of the Yom Kippur War* (Lexington, KY: University Press of Kentucky, 2014), p. 435.

14 Zeev Schiff, *October Earthquake: Yom Kippur 1973* (Tel Aviv: University Publishing Projects, 1974), p. 218.

15 Hanoch Bartov, *Dado, 48 Years and 20 Days: The Full Story of the Yom Kippur War and the Man Who Led Israel's Army* (Tel Aviv: Maariv Book Guild, 1981), p. 524. Bartov's account of the IDF chief of staff's part in the war is based upon transcripts of wartime conversations at IDF general headquarters (GHQ) and at the fronts, as well as on interviews with David Elazar's colleagues in the army and government.

16 Ibid., p. 559.

17 See the October 19 minutes of a WSAG meeting, Nixon Presidential Materials, NSC Files, NSC Institutional Files (H–Files), Box H–117, WSAG Meeting Minutes, Originals, 1973, National Archives. American officials reported that the IDF was pleased with the performance of these new weapons. On the accuracy and numbers of air-delivered PGMs employed by the IDF in the war, see William E. Depuy, "Implications of the Middle East War on U.S. Army Tactics, Doctrine, and Systems," in Richard M. Swaim, Donald L. Gilmore, and Carolyn D. Conway, *Selected Papers of General William E. DePuy* (Fort Leavenworth, KS: U.S. Army Command and Staff College, 1994), p. 92. General DePuy headed the American army's Training and Doctrine (TRADOC) Command during the Yom Kippur War, so he had access to information about the IDF's use of American-supplied PGMs.

18 Alistair Horne, *Hubris: The Tragedy of War in the Twentieth Century* (New York: HarperCollins, 2015), p. 342.

19 Herzog, *The War of Atonement*, p. 277.

8 The American Assessment

1. Saul Bronfeld, "Fighting Outnumbered: The Impact of the Yom Kippur War on the U.S. Army," *The Journal of Military History*, Vol. 71, No. 2 (April 2007), pp. 465–498.
2. To get a sense of the high-level exchanges between American and Israeli military officers after the Yom Kippur War, for example, see William E. DePuy, "Letter to General Frederick C. Weyand from General DePuy, August 18, 1976" in Richard M. Swain, Donald L. Gilmore, and Carolyn D. Conway, *Selected Papers of General William E. DePuy: First Commander, U.S. Army Training and Doctrine Command, 1 July 1973* (Fort Leavenworth, KS: U.S. Army Command and General Staff College 1994), pp. 199–205.
3. United States Army Military History Institute oral history interview conducted September 18, 1991 with Donn A. Starry. Douglas V. Johnson, Thomas Sweeney, and Douglas W. Craft, "Desert Storm Lessons Learned" in Lewis Sorley (ed.), *Press On!: Selected Works of General Donn A. Starry*, Vol. 2 (Fort Leavenworth, KS: U.S. Army Combined Arms Center, 2009), p. 1225.
4. United States Army War College/United States Army Military History Institute oral history interview conducted February 15–18, 1986 with Starry. Matthias A. Spruilli and Edwin T. Vernon, "Life and Career of General Donn A. Starry" in ibid., p. 1110.
5. Central Intelligence Agency. Directorate of Intelligence, *The 1973 Arab–Israeli War: Overview and Analysis of the Conflict* (Langley, VA: Central Intelligence Agency, 1975).
6. The most heavily redacted sections of the declassified report are "Comment on Sources" and "Bibliographical Note." Hence, one is not in a position to know which specific classified intelligence and military reports were consulted in its preparation. Given the substantial amount of text redacted in these sections, not to mention the copious amount of technical data in the report, however, it seems eminently sensible to conclude that a wide variety of classified reports was used in its preparation.
7. Interestingly, but not surprisingly, most of the handful of photographs in the report have also been deleted from the declassified version, probably to protect capabilities related to the gathering of VISINT, or visual intelligence, such as those possessed by satellites and high-altitude reconnaissance aircraft.
8. Directorate of Intelligence, *The 1973 Arab–Israeli War*, p. 49. Despite the fact that the report draws on authoritative American and Israeli sources, all of the figures cited in the document are best considered approximate rather than precise, as complete and reliable statistical information on the Yom Kippur War was not always available to American intelligence analysts and military officers at the time of publication.
9. Ibid., pp. 32–35.
10. Ibid., p. 43.

NOTES TO CHAPTER 8

11 Ibid., pp. 43–47.
12 Ibid., p. 32.
13 Ibid., p. 41.
14 William E. DePuy, "Letter to General Creighton Abrams from General DePuy, January 14, 1974" in Swain, Gilmore, and Conway, *Selected Papers*, p. 70.
15 On American pressure to refrain from a preemptive strike, see the October 6 telegram from Secretary of State Henry Kissinger to President Richard Nixon in Middle East War Memos and Miscellaneous (October 1–October 17), National Security Council (NSC) File, Nixon Presidential Materials, Box 664, National Archives, and the October 7 memorandum of conversation between Kissinger and Israeli Ambassador to the United States Simcha Dinitz in Records of Henry Kissinger, 1973–1977, Record Group 59, State Department Records, Box 25 (Category C 1973 Arab–Israeli War), National Archives. Also see Michael Brecher, *Decisions in Crisis: Israel, 1967 and 1973* (Berkeley: University of California Press, 1980), pp. 177–178, 187–188, and 197–201.
16 Steven J. Rosen and Martin Indyk, "The Temptation to Pre-empt in a Fifth Arab–Israeli War," *Orbis*, Vol. 20, No. 3 (Summer 1976), pp. 271–272. It should be mentioned that not all analysts are in agreement with this line of reasoning. For a dissenting opinion, see John R. Carter, *Airpower and the Cult of the Offensive* (Maxwell Air Force Base, AL: Air University Press, 1998), pp. 52–65.
17 In a June 25, 2007 conversation with the author at the Israel Air Force Center (IAFC), Herzliya, Israel, Brigadier General (Ret.) Itzhak Amitay, who flew many combat missions on the Sinai front during the war, confirmed that the Israel Air Force (IAF) was making progress against the Egyptian IADS before Israel Defense Forces (IDF) general headquarters (GHQ) stopped the operation in order to respond to the threat on the Golan. Also see Abraham Rabinovich, *The Yom Kippur War: The Epic Encounter that Transformed the Middle East* (New York: Schocken, 2004), pp. 175–180, and Emanuel Sakal, *Soldier in the Sinai: A General's Account of the Yom Kippur War* (Lexington, KY: University Press of Kentucky, 2014), pp. 338–342.
18 Directorate of Intelligence, *The 1973 Arab–Israeli War*, pp. 47–50.
19 Ibid., p. 50.
20 For more recent figures regarding IAF air-to-air victories and losses during the Yom Kippur War, for example, see David Rodman, *Sword and Shield of Zion: The Israel Air Force in the Arab–Israeli Conflict, 1948–2012* (Brighton: Sussex Academic Press, 2013), p. 32.
21 Directorate of Intelligence, *The 1973 Arab–Israeli War*, pp. 48–49.
22 William E. DePuy, "Implications of the Middle East War on U.S. Army Tactics, Doctrine and Systems," in Swain, Gilmore, and Conway, *Selected Papers*, pp. 91–92.
23 Directorate of Intelligence, *The 1973 Arab–Israeli War*, p. 53.

24 Ibid., pp. 54–64. The report also notes that the IDF's fixed defenses—a series of fortified strongpoints located on hilltops along the 1967 cease-fire line—played a significant role in the defense of the Golan by harassing Syrian supply columns, as well as by calling in artillery fire and air strikes against these targets.
25 Ibid., pp. 60–61 and 65.
26 Ibid., p. 57.
27 For the very different C^2 experiences of IDF forces on the Golan and in the Sinai, see Dani Asher et al., *Syrians at the Border: Strategies, Tactics, Battles, Israel's Northern Command, 1973* (Jerusalem: Contento de Semrik, 2014), and Sakal, *Soldier in the Sinai*, respectively.
28 Directorate of Intelligence, *The 1973 Arab–Israeli War*, pp. 62–64.
29 Johnson, Sweeny and Craft, "Desert Storm" in Sorely, *Press On!*, Vol. 2, p. 1227.
30 Directorate of Intelligence, *The 1973 Arab–Israeli War*, p. 65.
31 Ibid., pp. 67–68.
32 Ibid., pp. 76–77.
33 Ibid., pp. 74–78.
34 Directorate of Intelligence, *The 1973 Arab–Israeli War*, p. 81, and Sakal, *Soldier in the Sinai*, p. 174.
35 Directorate of Intelligence, *The 1973 Arab–Israeli War*, p. 71.
36 Ibid., p. 66.
37 Ibid., p. 82. See also William E. DePuy, "Letter to Senator John C. Culver from General DePuy, May 12, 1975" in Swain, Gilmore, and Conway, *Selected Papers*, p. 167. DePuy reaches the same conclusion as the CIA report. He states that, "In the later stages of the war (after the fourth or fifth day), [antitank missiles and rockets] ceased to play a significant role in the outcome of the battle. Once initial surprise wore off and [Israeli] tanks were employed according to established principles (combined arms team, proper use of terrain, and suppressive fire), the situation changed dramatically."
38 Sakal, *Soldier in the Sinai*, furnishes a massive critique of IDF C^2 problems in the Sinai during the first days of the war. Sakal served as a tank battalion commander on this front in the war, so he possesses great personal insight into these problems.
39 Ibid., pp. 208–284.
40 Ibid., pp. 208–284.
41 Directorate of Intelligence, *The 1973 Arab–Israeli War*, pp. 88–89.
42 Ibid., pp. 89–90.
43 Ibid., pp. 90–99.
44 Donn A. Starry, "Tanks Forever" in Lewis Sorley (ed.), *Press On!: Selected Works of General Donn A. Starry*, Vol. 1 (Fort Leavenworth, KS: U.S. Army Combined Arms Center, 2009), p. 50.
45 For a trenchant treatment of the American army's analysis of the war, see Bronfeld, "Fighting Outnumbered."

46 Directorate of Intelligence, *The 1973 Arab–Israeli War*, p. 107.
47 Ibid., p. 109.
48 Donn A. Starry, "Reflections" in Sorley, *Press On!*, Vol. 1, p. 26.
49 DePuy, "Letter to Senator John C. Culver" in Swain, Gilmore, and Conway, *Selected Papers*, p.166.
50 Directorate of Intelligence, *The 1973 Arab–Israeli War*, p. 108.
51 Ibid., p. 1. One senior TRADOC officer believed that less than 10 percent of IDF tank losses could actually be attributed to antitank missiles and rockets. Starry, "Reflections" in Sorley, *Press On!*, Vol. 1, p. 33.
52 DePuy, "Implications of the Middle East War" in Swain, Gilmore, and Conway, *Selected Papers*, p. 76.
53 Ibid., p. 79.
54 Ibid., p. 77.
55 Donn A. Starry, "TRADOC's Analysis of the Yom Kippur War" in Sorely, *Press On!*, Vol. 1, p. 222. Starry delivered this analysis as a lecture to a conference at Tel Aviv University's Jaffee Center for Strategic Studies on March 16, 1999.
56 DePuy, "Implications of the Middle East War" in Swain, Gilmore, and Conway, *Selected Papers*, p.76.
57 Starry, "TRADOC's Analysis" in Sorley, *Press On!*, Vol. 1, pp. 222–223.

9 The Israeli Response

1 For a brief overview of the Agranat Commission's findings and recommendations, see the entry about the commission at <www.knesset.gov.il>. Also see Emanuel Sakal, *Soldier in the Sinai: A General's Account of the Yom Kippur War* (Lexington, KY: University Press of Kentucky, 2014).
2 Uri Bar-Joseph, *The Watchman Fell Asleep: The Surprise of Yom Kippur and Its Sources* (Albany: SUNY Press, 2005), and Aryeh Shalev, *Israel's Intelligence Assessment Before the Yom Kippur War: Disentangling Deception and Distraction* (Brighton: Sussex Academic Press, 2010), both furnish meticulous accounts of A'MAN's shortcomings on the eve of the Yom Kippur War.
3 Alistair Horne, *Hubris: The Tragedy of War in the Twentieth Century* (New York: HarperCollins, 2015), pp. 340–341.
4 Chaim Bar Lev, "Surprise in the Yom Kippur War," in Louis Williams (ed.), *Military Aspects of the Israeli–Arab Conflict* (Tel Aviv: University Publishing Projects, 1975), p. 264.
5 For these statistics, see Anthony H. Cordesman and Abraham R. Wagner, *The Lessons of Modern War (Volume I): The Arab–Israeli Conflicts, 1973–1989* (Boulder, CO: Westview Press, 1990), pp. 110–112. Not only did the IDF double its stock of consumables, but it also moved them closer to the fronts so as to be able to get hold of them more quickly in an emergency.

6 David Elazar, "The Yom Kippur War: Military Lessons," in Williams, *Military Aspects of the Israeli–Arab Conflict*, p. 249.
7 Cordesman and Wagner, *The Lessons of Modern War*, pp. 110–112.
8 Elazar, "The Yom Kippur War," in Williams, *Military Aspects of the Israeli–Arab Conflict*, pp. 248–249.
9 Ibid., p. 249.
10 Cordesman and Wagner, *The Lessons of Modern War*, pp. 111–112.
11 For the experience of the Israel Navy (IN) in the Yom Kippur War, see Ze'ev Almog, *Flotilla 13: Israeli Naval Commandos in the Red Sea, 1967–1973* (Annapolis, MD: Naval Institute Press, 2010), and Abraham Rabinovich, *The Boats of Cherbourg: The Navy that Stole Its Own Boats and Revolutionized Naval Warfare* (New York: Henry Holt, 1988).
12 Elazar, "The Yom Kippur War," in Williams, *Military Aspects of the Israeli–Arab Conflict*, p. 259.
13 For a thorough review of the Lebanon War, see Cordesman and Wagner, *The Lessons of Modern War*, pp. 117–228.
14 The other accomplishment involved the destruction of the Egyptian, Jordanian, and Syrian air forces at the outset of the 1967 Six-Day War.
15 The IDF's harried withdrawal from the Beirut area, as well as its contentious presence in south Lebanon until mid-2000, reinforced this mindset.

Conclusion: From Defeat to Victory in the Yom Kippur War

1 Charles S. Liebman, "The Myth of Defeat: The Memory of the Yom Kippur War in Israeli Society," *Middle Eastern Studies*, Vol. 29, No. 3 (July 1993), p. 399.

Bibliography

Articles

Asher, Dani, "Time for the Next Generation," *Israel Defense*, No. 21 (July 2014).
Bendman, Yona and Yishai Cordova, "The Soviet Nuclear Threat Towards the Close of the Yom Kippur War," *The Jerusalem Journal of International Relations*, Vol. 5, No. 1 (March 1980).
Bolia, Robert S., "Overreliance on Technology in Warfare: The Yom Kippur War as a Case Study," *Parameters*, Vol. 34, No. 2 (Summer 2004).
Bronfeld, Saul, "Fighting Outnumbered: The Impact of the Yom Kippur War on the U.S. Army," *Journal of Military History*, Vol. 71, No. 2 (April 2007).
Cohen, Avner and William Burr, "Israel Crosses the Nuclear Threshold," *Bulletin of the Atomic Scientists*, Vol. 62, No. 3 (May 2006).
Greenbaum, Avraham, "The US Airlift to Israel in 1973 and Its Origins," *Israel Affairs*, Vol. 13, No. 1 (January 2007).
Levey, Zach, "Anatomy of an Airlift: United States Military Assistance to Israel During the 1973 War," *Cold War History*, Vol. 8, No. 4 (November 2008).
Liebman, Charles S., "The Myth of Defeat: The Memory of the Yom Kippur War in Israeli Society," *Middle Eastern Studies*, Vol. 29, No. 3 (July 1993).
Morrow, James D., "Alliances and Asymmetry: An Alternative to the Capability Aggregation Model of Alliances," *American Journal of Political Science*, Vol. 35, No. 4 (November 1991).
Pollack, Kenneth M., "Air Power in the Six-Day War," *The Journal of Strategic Studies*, Vol. 28, No. 3 (June 2005).
Raz, Adam, "The Significance of the Reputed Yom Kippur War Nuclear Affair," *Strategic Assessment*, Vol. 16, No. 4 (January 2014).
Rosen, Steven J. and Martin Indyk, "The Temptation to Pre-empt in a Fifth Arab–Israeli War," *Orbis*, Vol. 20, No. 3 (Summer 1976).

Books and Reports

Adan, Avraham (Bren), *On the Banks of the Suez: An Israeli General's Personal Account of the Yom Kippur War* (Novato, CA: Presidio Press, 1980).
Almog, Ze'ev, *Flotilla 13: Israeli Naval Commandos in the Red Sea, 1967–1973* (Annapolis, MD: Naval Institute Press, 2010).

BIBLIOGRAPHY

Aloni, Shlomo, *Ghosts of Atonement: Israeli F-4 Operations During the Yom Kippur War* (Atglen, PA: Schiffer Publishing, 2015).

Aloni, Shlomo, *The June 1967 Six-Day War (Volume A): Operation Focus* (Bat Hefer: Isradecal, 2008).

Aronson, Shlomo, *Conflict and Bargaining in the Middle East: An Israeli Perspective* (Baltimore: The Johns Hopkins University Press, 1978).

Aronson, Shlomo (with Oded Brosh), *The Politics and Strategy of Nuclear Weapons in the Middle East: Opacity, Theory, and Reality, 1960–1991* (Albany: State University of New York Press, 1992).

Asher, Dani, *The Egyptian Strategy for the Yom Kippur War: An Analysis* (Jefferson, NC: McFarland, 2009).

Asher, Dani et al., *Inside Israel's Northern Command: The Yom Kippur War on the Syrian Border* (Lexington, KY: University Press of Kentucky, 2016).

Asher, Dani et al., *Syrians at the Border: Strategies, Tactics, Battles, Israel's Northern Command, 1973* (Jerusalem: Contento de Semrik, 2014).

el Badri, Hassan, Taha el Magdoub, and Mohammed Dia el Din Zohdy, *The Ramadan War* (Fairfax, VA: HERO Books, 1978).

Bar-Joseph, Uri, *The Watchman Fell Asleep: The Surprise of Yom Kippur and Its Sources* (Albany: SUNY Press, 2005).

Bartov, Hanoch, *Dado, 48 Years and 20 Days: The Full Story of the Yom Kippur War and the Man Who Led Israel's Army* (Tel Aviv: Maariv Book Guild, 1981).

Bass, Warren, *Support Any Friend: Kennedy's Middle East and the Making of the U.S.–Israel Alliance* (New York: Oxford University Press, 2003).

Ben-Zvi, Abraham, *John F. Kennedy and the Politics of Arms Sales to Israel* (London: Routledge, 2002).

Ben-Zvi, Abraham, *Lyndon B. Johnson and the Politics of Arms Sales to Israel: In the Shadow of the Hawk* (London: Routledge, 2004).

Blum, Howard, *The Eve of Destruction: The Untold Story of the Yom Kippur War* (New York: Harper, 2003).

Boyne, Walter J., *The Two O'Clock War: The 1973 Yom Kippur Conflict and the Airlift that Saved Israel* (New York: Thomas Dunne Books, 2002).

Brecher, Michael, *Decisions in Crisis: Israel, 1967 and 1973* (Berkeley: University of California Press, 1980).

Brook, Itzhak, *In the Sands of Sinai: A Physician's Account of the Yom Kippur War* (Seattle: CreateSpace, 2012).

Carter, John R., *Airpower and the Cult of the Offensive* (Maxwell Air Force Base, AL: Air University Press, 1998).

Cohen, Avner, *Israel and the Bomb* (New York: Columbia University Press, 1998).

Cohen, Avner, *The Worst-kept Secret: Israel's Bargain with the Bomb* (New York: Columbia University Press, 2010).

Colby, Elbridge et al., *The Israeli "Nuclear Alert" of 1973: Deterrence and Signaling in Crisis* (Alexandria, VA: CNA, 2013).

Cordesman, Anthony H. and Abraham R. Wagner, *The Lessons of Modern War*

(Volume I): The Arab–Israeli Conflicts, 1973–1989 (Boulder, CO: Westview Press, 1990).
van Creveld, Martin, Steven L. Canby, and Kenneth S. Brower, *Air Power and Maneuver Warfare* (Maxwell Air Force Base, AL: Air University Press, 1994).
van Creveld, Martin, *Nuclear Proliferation and the Future of Conflict* (New York: The Free Press, 1993).
Daigle, Craig, *The Limits of Détente: The United States, the Soviet Union, and the Arab–Israeli Conflict, 1969–1973* (New Haven: Yale University Press, 2012).
Dayan, Moshe, *Moshe Dayan: Story of My Life* (New York: Warner Books, 1976).
Dowty, Alan, *Middle East Crisis: U.S. Decision Making in 1958, 1970, and 1973* (Berkeley: University of California Press, 1984).
Dunstan, Simon, *The Yom Kippur War: The Arab–Israeli War of 1973* (Oxford: Osprey Publishing, 2007).
Dupuy, Trevor N., *Elusive Victory: The Arab–Israeli Wars, 1947–1974* (New York: Harper and Row, 1978).
Eban, Abba, *Personal Witness: Israel Through My Eyes* (New York: Putnam, 1992).
el Gamasy, Mohammed, *The October War: Memoirs of Field Marshal El Gamasy of Egypt* (Cairo: American University of Cairo Press, 1993).
Gat, Moshe, *In Search of a Peace Settlement: Egypt and Israel Between the Wars, 1967–1973* (New York: Palgrave Macmillan, 2012).
Gawyrch, George W., *The Albatross of Decisive Victory: War and Policy Between Egypt and Israel in the 1967 and 1973 Arab–Israeli Wars* (Westport, CT: Praeger, 2000).
Golan, Matti, *The Secret Conversations of Henry Kissinger: Step-by-Step Diplomacy in the Middle East* (New York: Quadrangle, 1976).
Heikal, Mohammed, *The October War* (New York: Crown, 1980).
Heikal, Mohammed, *The Road to Ramadan* (New York: Ballantine Books, 1975).
Hersh, Seymour M., *The Samson Option: Israel's Nuclear Arsenal and American Foreign Policy* (New York: Random House, 1991).
Herzog, Chaim, *The War of Atonement: October, 1973* (Boston: Little, Brown and Co., 1975).
Holsti, Ole, P. Terrance Hopmann, and John D. Sullivan, *Unity and Disintegration in International Alliances* (New York: John Wiley & Sons, 1973).
House, Jonathan M., *Combined Arms Warfare in the Twentieth Century* (Lawrence, KS: University Press of Kansas, 2001).
Huth, Paul K., *Extended Deterrence and the Prevention of War* (New Haven: Yale University Press, 1988).
Israelyan, Victor, *Inside the Kremlin During the Yom Kippur War* (University Park, PA: Pennsylvania State University Press, 1995).

BIBLIOGRAPHY

Kahalani, Avigdor, *The Heights of Courage: A Tank Leader's War on the Golan* (Westport, CT: Praeger, 1984).

Karpin, Michael, *The Bomb in the Basement: How Israel Went Nuclear and What that Means for the World* (New York: Simon and Schuster, 2006).

Kegley, Charles W., Jr. and Gregory A. Raymond, *When Trust Breaks Down: Alliance Norms and World Politics* (Columbia, SC: University of South Carolina Press, 1990).

Kipnis, Yigal, *1973: The Road to War* (Charlottesville, VA: Just World Books, 2013).

Kissinger, Henry, *Crisis: The Anatomy of Two Major Foreign Policy Crises* (New York: Simon and Schuster, 2004).

Kreis, John F., *Air Warfare and Air Base Air Defense* (Washington, D.C.: United States Government Printing Office, 1988).

Kumaraswamy, P. R. (ed.), *Revisiting the Yom Kippur War* (Oxford: Routledge, 2000).

London Sunday Times, The Yom Kippur War (New York: Doubleday, 1974).

Luttwak, Edward N., *Strategy: The Logic of War and Peace* (Cambridge, MA: Harvard University Press, 1987).

McGrath, John J. (ed.), *An Army at War: Change in the Midst of Conflict* (Fort Leavenworth, KS: U.S. Army Command and General Staff College, 2005).

O'Ballance, Edgar, *No Victor, No Vanquished: The Yom Kippur War* (Novato, CA: Presidio, 1978).

Oren, Michael B., *Six Days of War: June 1967 and the Making of the Modern Middle East* (New York: Oxford University Press, 2002).

Orr, Ori, *These Are My Brothers: A Dramatic Story of Heroism During the Yom Kippur War* (Jerusalem: Contento de Semrik, 2013).

Palit, D. K., *Return to the Sinai: The Arab Offensive, October 1973* (New Dehli: Palit and Palit, 1974).

Parker, Richard B. (ed.), *The October War: A Retrospective* (Gainesville: University Press of Florida, 2001).

Pollack, Kenneth M., *Arabs at War: Military Effectiveness, 1948–1991* (Lincoln: University of Nebraska Press, 2002).

Pollock, David, *The Politics of Pressure: American Arms and Israeli Policy Since the Six Day War* (Westport, CT: Greenwood Press, 1982).

Quandt, William B., *Decade of Decisions: American Policy Toward the Arab–Israeli Conflict, 1967–1976* (Berkeley: University of California Press, 1977).

Rabinovich, Abraham, *The Boats of Cherbourg: The Navy that Stole Its Own Boats and Revolutionized Naval Warfare* (New York: Henry Holt, 1988).

Rabinovich, Abraham, *The Yom Kippur War: The Epic Encounter that Transformed the Middle East* (New York: Schocken, 2004).

Rodman, David, *Arms Transfers to Israel: The Strategic Logic Behind American Military Assistance* (Brighton: Sussex Academic Press, 2007).

Rodman, David, *Sword and Shield of Zion: The Israel Air Force in the Arab–Israeli Conflict, 1948–2012* (Brighton: Sussex Academic Press, 2013).

Sakal, Emanuel, *Soldier in the Sinai: A General's Account of the Yom Kippur War* (Lexington, KY: University Press of Kentucky, 2014).
Schelling, Thomas C., *Arms and Influence* (New Haven: Yale University Press, 1966).
Schiff, Ze'ev, *A History of the Israeli Army: 1874 to the Present* (New York: Macmillan, 1985).
Schiff, Ze'ev, *October Earthquake: Yom Kippur 1973* (Tel Aviv: University Publishing Projects, 1974).
Shalev, Aryeh, *Israel's Intelligence Assessment Before the Yom Kippur War: Disentangling Deception and Distraction* (Brighton: Sussex Academic Press, 2010).
Sharon, Ariel (with David Chanoff), *Warrior: The Autobiography of Ariel Sharon* (New York: Simon and Schuster, 1990).
el Shazly, Saad, *The Crossing of the Suez* (San Francisco: American Mideast Research, 1980).
Sheehan, Edward R. F., *The Arabs, Israelis, and Kissinger: A Secret History of American Diplomacy in the Middle East* (New York: Readers Digest Press, 1976).
Siniver, Asaf (ed.), *The Yom Kippur War: Politics, Diplomacy, Legacy* (New York: Oxford University Press, 2013).
Spiegel, Steven L., *The Other Arab–Israeli Conflict: Making America's Middle East Policy, from Truman to Reagan* (Chicago: The University of Chicago Press, 1986).
Vanitek, Boaz and Zaki Shalom, *The Nixon Administration and the Middle East Peace Process, 1969–1973: From the Rogers Plan to the Outbreak of the Yom Kippur War* (Brighton: Sussex Academic Press, 2013).
Walt, Stephen M., *The Origins of Alliances* (Ithaca: Cornell University Press, 1987).
Weiss, Ra'anan, *The Israeli AF in the Yom Kippur War: Facts and Figures* (Kfar Tavor: Isradecal, 2014).
Williams, Louis (ed.), *Military Aspects of the Israeli–Arab Conflict* (Tel Aviv: University Publishing Projects, 1975).

Primary Sources
Briefings, conversations, e-mail correspondence, and lectures by reserve or retired Israel Air Force (IAF) and active United States (USAF) officers.
Central Intelligence Agency. Directorate of Intelligence, *The 1973 Arab–Israeli War: Overview and Analysis of the Conflict* (Langley, VA: Central Intelligence Agency, 1975).
Howland, Nina and Craig Daigle (eds.), *Foreign Relations of the United States, 1969–1976*, Volume XXV, *Arab–Israeli Crisis and War, 1973* (Washington, D.C.: United States Government Printing Office, 2011). Many of the documents cited in the endnotes can be found in this volume.
Joint Technical Coordinating Group for Munitions Effectiveness, *Special*

BIBLIOGRAPHY

Report: Survey of Combat Damage to Tanks, Volumes I–III (Washington, D.C.: Defense Intelligence Agency, 1970).

Oral histories with United States Army Training and Doctrine (TRADOC) Command officers archived at the United States Military History Institute, Carlisle Barracks, Pennsylvania.

Sorley, Lewis (ed.), *Press On!: Selected Works of General Donn A. Starry*, Vol. 1 (Fort Leavenworth, KS: U.S. Army Combined Arms Center, 2009).

Sorley, Lewis (ed.), *Press On!: Selected Works of General Donn A. Starry*, Vol. 2 (Fort Leavenworth, KS: U.S. Army Combined Arms Center, 2009).

Swain, Richard M., Donald L. Gilmore, and Carolyn D. Conway, *Selected Papers of General William E. DePuy: First Commander, U.S. Army Training and Doctrine Command, 1 July 1973* (Fort Leavenworth, KS: U.S. Army Command and General Staff College, 1994).

United States Army. Department of Army Headquarters, *Army Doctrine Reference Publication No. 3–0: Unified Land Operations* (Washington, D.C.: Department of the Army Headquarters, 2012).

Various American and Israeli web sites.

Various State Department and White House records housed at the United States National Archives, College Park, Maryland.

Various TRADOC records housed at the United States Army Military History Institute, Carlisle Barracks, Pennsylvania.

Index

Agranat Commission, 113–115
airpower
    definitions of roles, 73–74
    impact on the Yom Kippur War, 53–55, 65–67, 71–85, 99–105
air superiority, 72–73, 81–82, 84
air supremacy, 73, 80, 84
alliance versus patron–client relationship, 13–14
A'MAN (IDF military intelligence), 5–7, 46, 114–115
American arms transfers
    during the Yom Kippur War, 7, 17–18, 21–22, 90–91
    impact on Golan front, 91–92
    impact on Sinai front, 93–95
    manipulation of, 21–22
    overall impact, 95–96, 116
    questions about, 89
American assessment of the Yom Kippur War
    airpower, 99–105
    basic lessons, 108–110
    Golan front, 103–105
    Sinai front, 105–107
American–Israeli relationship
    before the Yom Kippur War, 14–15
    during the Yom Kippur War, 15–24
    nature of, 13–14
    preemptive strike, 16–17, 21–23, 53, 66, 76–77, 90, 101–102, 135 n 24
    security-for-autonomy bargain, 13–14, 24
antiaircraft artillery (AAA), 46, 99–102, 107
antitank missiles and rockets (Arab), 51–52, 63, 68, 105–106, 109, 119, 153 n 37

asymmetrical alliance, definition of, 132–133 n 3

Bar Lev Line, 49–50, 61–63, 67, 105, 147 n 23

cargo flights, 17–18, 90
casualty evacuation, 74, 76, 80, 83
Central Intelligence Agency (CIA), 7, 9, 27, 60, 97–111
close air support (CAS), 71–73, 75–76, 78–79, 81–83, 100–101, 107, 109, 119–121
combined arms warfare
    basic lessons, 108–109, 118–119
    definition, 43
    examples, 43–44
    force structure, 43–44, 56
    on the Golan front, 47–49, 67–68
    on the Sinai front, 49–53, 67–68
    traditional, 44
    war-fighting doctrine, 43–44, 56
compellence, definition of, 139 n 8
"concept, the," 15, 45–46
"consumables," 17, 90, 116

Defense Condition (DEFCON), 37–38
deterrence, definition of, 138–139 n 5

Egypt–Israel peace treaty, 2, 115
electronic countermeasures (ECM), 77, 100, 117

few versus many, 108, 111, 116
force ratios at the outset of hostilities
    on the Golan front, 46, 103
    on the Sinai front, 46–47, 105

INDEX

"groupthink," definition of, 115

historiography of the Yom Kippur War
  diplomatic, 3–4
  military, 4–7

integrated air defense system (IADS), 46, 52–54, 66–68, 71–73, 77–78, 81, 83, 99–102, 109, 119–121
intelligence failure (Israeli), 7, 15–16, 114–115
interdiction, 71–73, 75–76, 78–79, 81–83, 100–101, 107, 109
Israel Air Force (IAF)
  air–ground cooperation, 53–55
  air-to-air combat, 78, 102, 147 n 19
  antitank helicopters, 120–121
  comparative performance in Six-Day and Yom Kippur Wars, 80–84
  early warning, 53
  "flying artillery," 45, 55, 67–68, 78
  "flying tanks," 120
  in the Six-Day War, 44, 74–76, 80–84
  in the Yom Kippur War, 65–67, 76–84, 99–103
  "loft" attacks, 100
  losses in the Yom Kippur War, 66, 99–102, 148 n 31
  number of sorties flown in Six-Day War, 75
  number of sorties flown in Yom Kippur War, 78
  post-Yom Kippur War, 117, 119–120
  preemptive strike, 16–17, 21–23, 53, 66, 76–77, 90, 101–102, 135 n 24
Israel Defense Forces (IDF)
  airpower, 53–55, 65–67, 71–85, 99–103
  combined arms warfare, 41–57, 67–68, 108–109, 118–119
  command and control (C^2), 51, 55, 60, 63–64, 69, 74, 79, 104, 106, 111–112, 118, 126
  criticisms of, 41–42, 56

  on the Golan front, 47–49, 67–68, 91–92, 103–105
  on the Sinai front, 49–53, 67–68, 93–95, 105–107
  post-Yom Kippur War, 116–121
  reserve mobilization, 48, 50, 64–65
  surrounds Egyptian Third Army, 18–19, 22–23, 37, 55, 93, 107
  versus Jordanian army, 30–31, 104–105
Israel–Jordan peace treaty, 2, 115
Israel Navy (IN), 7, 57, 117, 120–122
Israeli–Jordanian relationship
  before the Yom Kippur War, 27–28
  during the Yom Kippur War, 25–27, 28–31
Israeli response to the Yom Kippur War
  IDF force structure reforms, 116–118
  IDF war-fighting doctrine reforms, 118–121
  intelligence reforms, 114–116

Jordan River, 25–26
Jordan Valley, 25–26
Jordanian civil war (1970), 14, 26–27
Judea and Samaria, 25, 72, 75

"kill ratio" (air-to-air combat), 102

Lebanon War (1982), 121–122
logistical support, 74, 76, 80, 84

Maginot Line, 105
maneuver versus attrition warfare, 140 n 6
Military Airlift Command (MAC), 91
Mount Hermon, 49, 64, 80, 104

National Security Agency (NSA), 27
North Atlantic Treaty Organization (NATO), 2, 13, 97, 99, 104, 108
"No war, no peace," 14
Nuclear Nonproliferation Treaty (NPT), 34
nuclear weapons
  American, 19, 37–38
  Israeli, 33–37

Operation Cast Lead, 123
Operation Challenge 4, 77, 101–102
Operation Focus, 74–75
Operation Model 5, 77, 101–102
Operation Protective Edge, 123
operational level of warfare, 6, 44, 52, 97

petroleum, oil, lubricants (POL), 73, 79, 116, 120
precision-guided munition (PGM), 95, 102, 109, 117, 121, 150 n 17

quantity versus quality, 116–118

reconnaissance, 74, 76, 80, 84

Second Lebanon War (2006), 84, 123
Sinai Campaign (1956), 121, 129 n 1
"sitzkrieg," 107
Six-Day War (1967), 1, 14, 16, 20, 25, 33, 41–42, 57, 67, 71, 74–76, 79–84, 90, 99, 114, 121, 129 n 1
small-unit leadership, 103, 108
strategic attack, 72–73, 79
Suez Canal, 1, 6, 49, 53, 59–61, 78, 93, 107
surface-to-air missile (SAM) batteries, 46, 54, 77–78, 80, 99–102, 107, 119

tactical level of warfare, 6, 44, 52, 97
"tank charges," 50–51, 67, 105
Training and Doctrine (TRADOC) Command, 56, 97–98, 104, 107–110

troop transport, 73–74, 76, 79–80, 83

unmanned aerial vehicle (UAV), 77, 117–118, 121

War of Attrition (1969–70), 14, 20, 84, 129 n 1
War of Independence (1947–9), 129 n 1
Warsaw Pact (WP), 2, 97, 99, 104, 108

Yom Kippur War (1973)
  airpower, 53–55, 65–67, 71–73, 76–85, 99–105
  American arms transfers, 89–96
  American assessment, 97–111
  American–Israeli relationship, 13–24
  basic lessons, 108–110
  battlefield topography, 51, 60–62
  casualties and losses, 2, 41, 66, 99–102, 109, 125, 148 n 31
  combined arms warfare, 41–57, 67–68, 118–119
  effect on Israeli psyche, 125–126
  Golan front, 47–49, 67–68, 91–92, 103–105
  historiography, 3–7
  IDF reserve mobilization, 48, 50, 64–65
  Israeli response to, 113–123
  Sinai front, 49–53, 67–68, 93–95, 105–107

About the Author

David Rodman is the author of three previous volumes about Israel: *Sword and Shield of Zion: The Israel Air Force in the Arab–Israeli Conflict, 1948–2012*; *Arms Transfers to Israel: The Strategic Logic Behind American Military Assistance*; and *Defense and Diplomacy in Israel's National Security Experience: Tactics, Partnerships, and Motives*, all Sussex Academic Press books. He has also published articles in professional journals, including *Intelligence and National Security*, *The Journal of Strategic Studies*, *Middle Eastern Studies*, *Israel Affairs*, *MERIA Journal*, *Defence Studies*, and *Israel Journal of Foreign Affairs*.

www.ingramcontent.com/pod-product-compliance
Lightning Source LLC
Chambersburg PA
CBHW071411300426
44114CB00016B/2259